Understanding the Far-Reaching Global Impact of the World Racial Order

Sterlin Williams

Stew Books Publishing—Southaven, MS
ISBN: 978-1-7335893-0-7
Library of Congress Control Number: 2019900413
Title: *Understanding the Far-Reaching Global Impact of the World Racial Order*
Author: Sterlin Williams
Digital distribution | 2019
Paperback Edition

Published in the United States by New Book Authors Publishing—Madison, WI.

Dedication

To the memory of my parents, Eunice and Dorothy M. Williams, siblings, Evester L. Darrough and Charles L. Williams, and Dr. Steven M. Neuse, MPA Director of the University of Arkansas who challenged me to think critically and analytically in problem solving.

About The Author

Sterlin Dwayne Williams is a native of Pine Bluff, Arkansas. Sterlin had a successful career with the Federal Motor Carrier Safety Administration (U.S. Department of Transportation) and retired after thirty-two years of federal service. During his career, he served as the Division Administrator for twenty-six years for the states of Louisiana and Mississippi. He was responsible for the statewide implementation of federal interstate motor carrier safety/economic/hazardous materials programs where he partnered with numerous partners and stakeholders.

While with the agency, Sterlin served as the first chairperson of the National Diversity Committee. Because of his leadership, he received the agency's Diversity Champion Award and the Secretary of Transportation's Equal Employment Opportunity (EEO) and Affirmative Action Award in directing and implementing the agency's Diversity Initiative.

Sterlin attended Dollarway High School and received his Bachelor of Science in Business Administration and Master of Public Administration at the University of Arkansas in Fayetteville, Arkansas. His interests include art, traveling, golf, sports and reading. He is a member of the Alpha Phi Alpha fraternity, Inc.

Contents

Acknowledgements

I must first give thanks to the ancestors in whose path that we follow paved the way for us. It is now our duty to set an example for those who follow us.

A book of this magnitude written at this stage of my life after completing my work career could not have been accomplished without the contributions of many trusted friends and associates who touched and shaped my life at some point. The contents of this book are not just about my opinions about the subject matter but theirs as well along with many other people from all walks of life. My heartfelt appreciation to all. However, there are a few whose mention must be especially noted.

Special thanks to my wife, Priscilla Samuels Williams, my daughter, Alexis Shennell Williams, sisters Dr. Bettye J. Williams and Dr. Brenda F. Graham, and my mother in law, Martha L. Samuels for their comments, feedback, candid critique and appraisal of the manuscript that made it a reality.

To all my siblings, Evester L. Darrough (decreased), Dr. Bettye J. Williams, Shirley M. Williams, Dr. Brenda F. Graham, Dr. Margarette A. Williams and Lewis J. Williams, Charles L. Williams (decreased), N. Lucille Gilkey, Ted W. Williams, Robin N. Baylock, and Sonnya N. Adams and Dwight Adams Sr. for your inspiration over the years. To all my nephews, nieces, great-nephews, great-nieces, aunts, uncles, cousins and friends for always supporting me.

Sincere thanks to Richard Bullard, Barry Turner, Victor A. Wilson and Michael Woolfolk for their unbiased valued comments throughout the years in our debates of this subject matter and many others whose opinions heavily contributed in the unstinting support of my aspiration to make this book possible.

Toni Morrison, a noted American writer, educator and editor who received the Nobel Prize for Literature in 1993 has been credited with the remarks, "if there's a book you want to read, but it hasn't been written yet, you must write it." The subject matter in this book has been a topic that I along with many people throughout the world experience.

This book is a culmination of a path that I have been on since I was a child. Many years later as an adult, I was able to survey my current surroundings and environment. The totality of my life's experiences prepared me to write this book.

There is a lot of good information available on global racism, but the overall body of knowledge was in a piece-meal fashion. Hopefully, this book can fill the key gaps in understanding how our world is presently constructed in race relations. I wanted to share this information with others who are facing the same dilemma in our ongoing effort to achieve racial equality.

Introduction

The term 'new world order' is a major subject whose ideology has been around for millennia but was recently resurrected by some twenty and twenty first centuries world leaders and governments. Its basic ideology is an assembly of nations coming together for mutual benefit to come up with one world government, religion, currency, army, police, race, and others. Some people have called the concept a plot or conspiracy theory developed by a secret underground society or others who work behind the scenes to take over the world. However, the concept has been recently discussed and debated by many world leaders and some of its basic concepts have already been used around the world.

This book will address the 'world racial order.' This order exists because of the fifteenth century decision by several European countries to conquer, colonize and enslave most of the world. This led to the (1) genocide of the indigenous people in the Americas, Africa, parts of Asia, Australia, New Zealand and other parts of the world, (2) the colonization of most of the world's countries and (3) the enslavement of Africans in the Americas and the Caribbean. Its legacy is still felt today and is the primary reason for the existence of the racial order that exists today. This order caused a major reverberation of race relationships on a global scale.

This book will not address the concepts of the 'new world order' although the one race concept is very intriguing. However, it will discuss the recent racial global issues from a social, economic, political and cultural perspective. Several very important major events occurred since the end of the Transatlantic Slave Trade in the late 1800's. These world events have transformed racism on a global scale and reset the trajectory of how world's systems and institutions will deal with race in the future.

Further, this book will provide some insights to the dominant racial groups so that they can have some empathy for those members of the subordinate groups and actively work to change or reform the institutions and systems that have cause these social ills. More importantly, the book can serve as the catalyst for the dominant racial groups to learn more about global racial inequalities and to work for global racial justice to make amends for wrongdoings of the past.

Although racism will never be completely eradicated in the world, there are still strategies that members of the subordinate groups can incorporate in their lives to ensure that their existence in the world are still meaningful so that they can reach their full potential. If they don't truly understand racism as a global dynamic of survival for power by the dominant cultures, then proper strategies cannot be developed to combat the problem of various ills destroying the marginalized communities around the world.

Finding solutions to the problems will not be easy. Racism is an extremely difficult and complex social issue. It is almost impossible to nail down because it is both systemic and pervasive. It can be deliberate and unintentional. It is destructive, cruel, belittles, and humilities its victims. Sometimes it is difficult to prove because racism lies deep within the soul of one's character. However, throughout humankind, it has been quietly held in a society's histories, institutions, systems and public policies.[i]

Although progress has been made during the past few decades, there are still a lot of unresolved global racial issues. All racial groups can overcome these challenges by first educating themselves on the real history of worldwide Colonialism and the Transatlantic Slave Trade and its aftermath during this existing world racial order. As a result of the Transatlantic Slave Trade and worldwide Colonialism, global racial issues have become very complicated during the past five centuries. Racism is so intertwined with other global policy issues that it's sometimes difficult to untangle race from other public policy concerns.

The closing purpose of this book is to help all members of the human race gain an understanding of the systemic pervasive epidemic of racism and how it is presently constructed on a global scale. I will review the impact and the historical complex origins of global racism and discuss how racism was formulated during the existing world racial order. I will identify past and present global racial inequalities, discuss the implication of global racial transformation and the resetting of global change. Finally, I will discuss ways to achieve global racial justice and sustainability. Hopefully a greater understanding and awareness of the dynamics and interactions that the various racial groups experience can bring about an era of atonement and redemption. This understanding will allow the various global racial groups and members of the human race to live and exist in harmony.

PART ONE – THE IMPACT OF GLOBAL RACISM

My whole life has been mostly defined by race and my entire existential reality has been shaped by the context and standards of the dominant culture. As I enter my sixth decade in this world, I still grapple daily with racial issues just during routine activities that members of other racial groups take for granted. For example, as an adult, if I shop at upscale stores, I am conscious of being watched very closely by store personnel who think that I plan to steal something. I am seen as leery and untrustworthy. I have experienced several conflicts with some members of the dominant culture in all the integrated neighborhoods, I have ever lived in. Some of these conflicts with neighbors have not been subtle and a few have let me know directly that I was not welcomed in the neighborhood. During my work career, I had to deal with the constant realities and challenges of racial microaggressions which some people of color experience in a predominantly white workplace when they are a racial minority. When I drive my automobile, I have to constantly remind, myself to strictly observe all traffic laws or I may be stopped by a policeman who has a quota to fill and I'm the easy victim who is powerless in society.

As a child, I had my first direct experience with racism at the age of seven. I still have a scar on my forehead from that racial incident that required several stitches to physically heal. It was from an encounter with white male occupancies driving an automobile who threw whiskey glass bottles at me and my brother when we were walking home one evening. They also called us the N-word when they sped past us and tried to run us off the road. Also, while in elementary school at a predominately white school before integration officially started in the United

1

States as the only student of African descent in the class, I was called the N-word in the fifth grade by a white female student sitting directly behind me in my Arkansas history class.

The list of personal experiences in my lifetime dealing with racism, discrimination, prejudice, being stereotyped and the subject of biases are very long. Each time it happens, the experience gets deeper and more intense. Over a period of time, it slowly takes a psychologically, emotional and physical toll on you.

The reason I along with billions of people of color experience these daily slights is because we are simply at the bottom of the global racial order culturally, socially, politically and economically. If subordinate group members live in a pluralistic society, their experiences may be slightly different than mine, but each has his own. Presently, whites sit at the top of the dominant culture. Asians sit in second place, and their influence is gaining in each decade. Brown and indigenous people are in third place and black people or those of African descent are in last place.

Global racism is a worldwide, complex social phenomenon. It is a global system of power privileges by the dominant cultures. The members of subordinate groups have relatively low power, prestige and economic position in a society's system of social stratification. Not only this, they have to observe the norms, values, cultural patterns and laws of the dominant culture.[ii] Global racism will never be completely eradicated but its current implications on the impacted subordinate groups can be minimized. Throughout the history of humankind, racism and prejudices by different racial groups pitted against others and even within their own racial groups have been deeply entrenched, permeated and embedded in all the segments and fabric of the world's societies. Racism divides the world's societies and fractures the idea of a common global hood.

Presently whites are at the top of the global racial order but in the past other racial groups were on top of the pecking order.

Asians are widely respected as a close second on the pecking order. Both racial groups on the top of the present racial order have a long history in their racism and prejudices toward people of darker skins.[iii] On the other hand, there are racism and prejudice among all the racial groups even within their own groups, albeit in a somewhat lesser degree.

The decline of the Chinese civilization propelled the Europeans to take over the top spot through the advent of the Transatlantic Slave Trade in the fifteenth century. China and India were world's economic powerhouses as late as the 1700's. Neither country had a culture of colonizing other countries. India had no tradition of sea faring and was colonized by the British because of their disorganized kingdoms. The balance of power shifted during that time due to religious, cultural and social changes. China had a rich culture but placed less emphasis on sea fearing and exploration. They did, however, learn from India's mistakes and were not colonized by the British.[iv]

We live in a global society where individual, institutional and cultural racism permeates all areas of our culture in an ever-expanding manner. Institutional racism is the most pervasive and powerful expression and form of racism. Because most people carry out their lives within institutions, control of institutions affects people's life choice. This does not mean that the dominant group is the majority group in terms of numbers. A small dominant group can still hold power over the majority. Even in places where subordinate groups are the majority such as South Africa before Apartheid ended and Ferguson, Missouri, they are still discriminated by pre-structured practices, public polices and power arrangements.

Individual racism relates to the joint operation of personal stereotypes, prejudices, and discrimination to create and support disparities between members of different racial groups. An example is endorsement of statements about innate group difference, the relatively inferiority of subordinate group members and policies that reinforces group differences in the distribution of resources.[v]

Institutional racism refers to intentional or unintentional manipulation or toleration of institutional policies (poll taxes, admissions criteria, attempts to limit subordinate group's voting power, limiting immigration on the basis of assumptions about the inferiority of subordinate groups) that unfairly restrict the opportunities of subordinate racial groups. Institutional racism involves the differential effects of policies, practices and laws on members of subordinate group members.[vi]

Cultural racism occurs when the dominant culture exerts the power to define cultural values for the society. Cultural racism involves not only a preference for the culture, heritage and values of one's own group but also the imposition of this culture on subordinate groups. The consequences of cultural racism are that subordinate groups are encouraged and sometime forced to turn their back on their own culture and to become assimilated into the dominant culture.[vii]

During my lifetime, there have been lot of presumptions about race that has been absolved without questioning, particularly by some members of the descendants of the dominant culture group. Some have been in a state of denial and refuse to deal with the issue of race. Some develop opinions about race from their culture that do not provide them informed opinions and multiple perspectives. Some ignore the vast amount of historical and contemporary evidence detailing how society is politically, economically and socially structured toward their advantage. They have never personally experienced institutional racism in their entire lives. They are not directly impacted so indifference and apathy set in.

The experiences of the dominant culture communities are structured and shaped in ways that distort their perception of

4

reality versus other racial groups. Their life's experiences have been just the opposite of those at the bottom of the racial social order. They are universal respected, revered and pander to by all the other racial groups in every corner of the globe. This has made some of them oblivious, ignorant and insensitive to the racial issues and plight that people with darker skin experience. They look as their life experiences as the norm and can't comprehend or refuse to comprehend why other racial groups don't feel the same way. They have been indoctrinated since birth and their biases are so deeply ingrained in them that they don't realize the depth of their racism. Their socialization renders them racially illiterate.

But deep down inside, some of them are aware of past histories and injustices that have happened to the other racial groups. They just refuse to get involved with the injustices they see and hear about because of peer pressure they may receive from other members of their racial group. Also, those injustices can become complicated and messy and they say it makes them feel 'uncomfortable' so some just choose to remain silent. Some don't want to face those issues; therefore, they avoid having the tough conversation on race. Also, some don't want to deal with anything that may impact the special status that they presently receive in society, so they just ignore the pleas for justice and do nothing. It helps them maintain their cultural distinctiveness and group solidarity.

The power of culture cannot be denied in that it helps shapes us. "Culture is the way of life of a group of people. It is a social heritage that is learned and shared by the group. Culture provides a basis for common understanding and cooperation among people in society. It dictates that we and others like us who learn and share the same social heritage will have basically the same initial outlook on life, that all of us will think, feel, and act at least initially, in a certain manner."[viii] The dominant culture in society rarely if ever admits to its own racism and the denial is usually universal. That is why many nations rarely offer any official apologies or issue repreparations to victims. They have a vested interest only in their privileges.[ix]

For those who have been the victims of global racism, the quest for answers to enhance their humanity has been the driving force and passion that animates the lives of many. They are aware that due to the special favors that the racial groups at the top of the racial social order receives, their lives are devalued. It is traumatic to live their life and at some point find out that everything they have been told about their existence has been fabricated. For some, it has caused them to reject their environment and upbringings and seek answers to discover their true roots and heritages. Many had to endure the psychological trauma of undoing their education and upbringings that they had previously lived with. The propaganda from the dominant culture on their life's experiences has caused them to re-orientate their religions, education, values, culture, heritages and identities.

Some members of the dominant cultures have no clue about the lives of members of the subordinate groups nor do some want to know. People never give up power, wealth, or privilege voluntarily in a society and share with others. As a person of color, experiences in my travels around the world have shaken my confidence in the world meeting its social obligations in good faith to other people who share my skin tone. I know that all human beings do not feel this way, so this means our world still has a lot of work to do in race relations.

Racism is a man-made invention. People whose skin have lighter skin tones have historically considered themselves superior to those with darker skin tones. They gain tremendous social status on the simple basis of being lighter than their darker skin brethren. Lighter skin tones have global market value whereas the darker your skin, you lose value in the world market. Labels and colors were created by human beings to create a worldwide racial social order. The color of black has been given a negative stigma of worthlessness and degradation[x] and synonymous with bad things by the dominant cultures.

Human beings, like all other species, display a wide range of inherited physical characteristics. Members of African descent have distinctive physical features and the most obvious differences of skin tone than other racial groups, particularly members of the dominant group. "These involuntary ethnic characteristics make them easily identifiable targets of discrimination. They face considerably more formidable obstacles to success and acceptance than do members of ethnic groups whose ethnic characteristics are all, voluntary – that is, those individuals who are not physically distinguishable from the dominant culture group."[xi]

Millennia has passed but it appears that the tribal instincts in early humans have not changed today. In general, racism that began with tribalism in early humans appears to be at the root of the race problem. The ancient world had homogenous societies that discriminated against each other on the bases of tribalism. Early humankind had biases against different tribes or ethnic groups within their confined geographical areas. Later, during the Transatlantic Trade Slave in the fifteenth century and worldwide Colonialism, those biases were spread to all areas of the globe.

The human nature and tribal instinct of early humans tended to want to cast people who were not part of their tribe as better then members of other tribes. The tribal members developed fear and anxiety; envy and resentment; ignorance and arrogance toward other tribal members. This type of socialization impairs the normal empathy or compassion that generally prevents people from casually harming their fellow human beings. Although we no longer live in such societies, we did for most of our existence on this planet. The fear of those who look, speak, or act differently from our racial group may be an epigenetic holdover from our ancient past.[xii] This fear was a survival mechanism that in the modern world became misconstrued as certain forms of prejudice or racism.

Social scientist and anthropologists are far from accurate in pinpointing the specific timeline and details of human evolution. A consensus exists, however, that human beings that we know of today appeared rather late in the evolutionary development. Obviously, we have not evolved sufficiently in the twenty-first century as human beings for some to understand that another ethnic group with different genetic makeup and lineage is not necessarily a threat to their existence and survival or inferior to your culture.

Unfortunately, the present major stigma of global racism is the color of one's skin because it's so easily identifiable by the naked eye. Even if society eliminates the stigma of one's color, early tribal instincts in humans would find other stigmas to feel superior or supreme to another group of people. It may be the color of one's eyes, hair color, their religion, nationality, anti-Semitism, and others. Racism has an appetite that cannot be quenched.

In many cases, racism has stripped Africa Americans of their true identities, names, heritages, cultures and religions where they were forced to Christianize. My heritage is from West Africa, but I have no idea of my real African family tree and limited knowledge of my American family tree. My genealogical DNA tests came back with conflicting results, so I only know the region in Africa where I originated from. I don't even know the names of my ancestors in West Africa or the country they reside in. The dominant racial group does not deal with the total loss of their identities.

Generally, Asians, African Americans and Hispanics are not getting the same specificity of ethnicity estimates as European-Americans from their genealogical DNA tests. The tests based on

8

the size of the reference database in which the availability of sample size can pinpoint where your ancestors came from. In the past, most companies used European-centric samples because they were easier to get and where many of their customers' ancestors came from. In November 2018, Ancestry.com published a listing of people in its reference panels for each region. The Germanic Europe panel included 2,072 people, while there was just 65 from Western and Central India and 41 from North Africa.

African Americans had a distinct challenge of sample sizes because of the Transatlantic Slave Trade. During slavery, many records were lost or destroyed. Thus, limited or no physical records were available for analysis. A conundrum exists for those looking to trace non-European roots because the DNA test hundreds of thousands of locations of a person's genome with databases of known DNA samples. However, more subordinate racial groups are requesting DNA test every year thus adding to the reference panels and deepened their pool of connections that is used to establish baseline ethnicities. Most companies are constantly adding to their panels and algorithms which will increase the specificity of ethnicity estimates in the future.[xiii]

Without your cultural identity, you can become anything the dominant culture wants you to be. There is nothing we haven't tried to assimilate into the dominant culture. In every epoch of the world societies, Africans and African Americans have shown their humanity in every sector; however, because of their genetic makeup and lineage, they are still devalued as individuals and as a racial group. There is no amount of assimilation that can shield you from racism in some pluralistic societies. Sometimes, it is difficult to break free of the of the ways of the dominant hegemony and forge your own path.

When Europeans migrated to America from the various countries in Europe, all of them had ambivalent racial status in the United States society. Over time, the strategy of positioning the different European nationalities with the 'white' label against members of the subordinate groups was successful. They considered themselves as white, no matter what European country they migrated from and more importantly, they came to be considered white by their fellow Americans. Prior to migrating to America from Europe, they were labeled by their nationalities.[xiv] This privilege would position them in the dominant culture to be culturally, politically, socially and economically advantaged than people of color.

These labels and identifications that nullify one's existence and place another one in a higher position on society's racial social order based solely on one attribute of a person's genetic makeup and lineage is a platform by which the vehicle of history is plying same path of those well trident roads of the past. Life is worth living when the act of dehumanizing one another is stopped. "To have problems in life is an inherent part of the human condition. But it takes self-examination, humility, grace and empathy to take the time and space to truly understand that some racial groups of the human race truly have it much better than others."[xv] As civilized human beings, we should not be dealing with the folly of racism.

This whole premise of the dominant culture supremacy is faulty from the beginning because no person should be defined by a group or race. We are all individuals and part of the human race. Most of us have blood lines from various racial or ethnicity groups. The average African American for example had genes that were only 73.2 percent African. Europeans genes accounted for 24 percent of their DNA, while .8 percent came from Native Americans. On the other hand, a 2014 New York Times report that said "European-Americans had genomes that were on average 98.6 percent European, .19 percent African, and .18 Native American. Latinos had genes that were on average 65.1 percent European, 18 percent Native American, and 6.2 percent African.[xvi]

Race is a made-up condition. There is a consensus among scientists that all humans originated and descended from Africa some of whom migrated and settled in Europe, Asia and to other places around the world. This has been demonstrated anthropologically as well as with the genetic record. Genetically, we are all identical. Our skin color, over time has changed depending on the region of the world where we live. A mutation in one of our genes is responsible for our skin color. The real problems arise when those differences between the racial groups are seen as an excuse to favor one racial group over another one.

There are reasons for the physical differences among racial groups. "The main reason for differences in physical appearance among our ancestors, from who we inherited our physical appearances, is successful adaptation to local environments. Since environments differed with respect to temperature, altitude, topography, humidity, and available food supply, and in various other ways, different physical traits were conducive to survival in different locations. Conversely, other traits were nonadaptive, and people who had them died with reproducing. Given the tendency in nature toward extreme variability, something resembling the full range of genes exists in all populations. However, the frequency of traits varies according to the local environment. Formerly impenetrable barriers such as mountains, deserts, forests, and oceans isolated human populations from each other for many thousands of years, thus allowing natural selection to create racial differences.[xvii]

Race is not based on science. However, it has been used to subjugate people who were different from those who proposed these fallacies regarding the superiority of themselves. "The 1997 President's Initiative on Race elicited numerous comments regarding its intent and focus. One such comment was made by Jefferson Fish, a psychologist at St. John's University in New York, who said: "This dialogue on race is driving me up the wall.

Nobody is asking the question, 'What is race?' It is a biologically meaningless category". Biologists, geneticists, and physical anthropologists, among others, long ago reached a common understanding that race is not a "scientific" concept rooted in discernible biological differences. Thus, although race may have no biological meaning, as used in reference to human differences, it has an extremely important and highly contested social one."[xviii]

During early human history, the term 'race' was used to describe people and societies in terms we use today as ethnicity or national identity. Later, during the Transatlantic Slave Trade in the fifteenth century, race was given a biological meaning which has now been debunked. The term 'race' is different then 'ethnicity'. 'Races' are distinguished by physical characteristics, which are thought to be fixed whereas 'ethnicities" by perceived ancestry, history, and cultural practices. Although ethnicity and nationality often overlap, a nationality of a group of people belonging to a nation such as American, can contain many ethnic groups such as African-American, Italian-Americans or Arab-Americans. ` The terms are social constructs and shaped by political power, group interest and other social and cultural forces.[xix]

Racism has been used to conquer, colonize, enslave and inferiorize some people with darker skin tones socially, culturally, and juridically, denigrate their culture and impose the oppressor's cultures and standards for all human beings. Racism is not just an individual's intentional hatred, bigotry, words and deeds towards others. It may also be an implicit and subconscious biases as well. The concept of racism has been used to justify and prescribe the exploitation, domination and violence against darker skin brethren. They justify their conquests of other racial groups and the exploiting of their land as normal and in tune with the natural order of the universe in which there is a survival of the fittest concept where one racial group is superior over other racial groups.

12

The European powers also used this concept to divide global political boundaries. When the Europeans colonized Africa, they drew up political boundaries to gain control over the lands. They were not interested in how the boundaries impacted the African people. A group of people that didn't get along with each other were placed in the same political boundaries which caused conflict and tribal wars. The Europeans drew up these boundaries based on what would help them and not on what was good for the Africans.

During the Transatlantic Slave Trade in the fifteenth century and worldwide Colonialism that led to our existing world racial order, the European powers took advantages of other world's cultures who were different from theirs and not as advanced as theirs in the sense as to what modernization and technology is today. The cultures of the indigenous people and their traditional life style were thought to be misunderstood, underappreciated and inferior to the European culture. The Europeans, through Colonialism, acquired full or partial political control of these countries, occupying it with their settlers, and exploiting it economically.

Race, which leads to racism led to slavery, global Colonialism, Apartheid and the Holocaust. Racial ideology runs deep in our history and culture and is the lenses through which we interpret these inequalities. In order to enslave a person, you have to come the conclusion that he is less than human. In the case of Transatlantic Slave Trade, the institution of slavery was established under the assumption that the Africans were not as human as Europeans were. And thus, the African lives were devalued and considered inferior. Africans were thought to be suitable for slavery instead of something more akin to the system of indentured servitude which some Europeans were part of. The indigenous people were first considered as slaves, but they were found to be unsuited for it. It would have been unthinkable to create slaves out of even the lowliest French, Italian or British citizen within the American Colonies. Thus, racism gave permission to utilize a specific racial group as chattel, under the guise of them being less than human for economic gain.

Throughout human history, slavery and racism have always existed but somewhat independently of each other. Both concepts, however, come from a sort of cultural or class arrogance by the perpetrators. In most cases, slavery involved tribalism and opportunism. The earliest examples of slavery refer to slaves drawn from within a population that requires slaves: usually indigents and criminals were taken. Once those people were depleted, the societies began taking slaves from tribes or group they conquered in open warfare. But even in those situations, there was a demand within the societies that depended on more slaves. "Because conflicts occurred between neighboring peoples, the slave population did not differ racially in any significant way from the master population. Before the European invasion, there had not been a racial basis to world slavery."[xx]

Only recently during the Transatlantic Slave Trade during the fifteenth century did European-American begin to rely almost exclusively on members of another society. It was the people from the continent of Africa. This along with modern slavery, latent seeds of racism that do exist in relationship to slavery and began to attain some measure of racial dominance involving the doctrine of inferiority and superiority of the human race.

Historically, the disenfranchisement of groups of people was primarily based on class and social status during previous empires, civilizations or societies. Europeans-Americans propagated the disenfranchisement of people based solely on one attribute of a person's genetic makeup and lineage. Although slavery was neither new nor unique to America, the modern concept of racial superiority or inferiority is a social construct of America.

Anytime you treat a group of people as property or something to be used and then discard them when they cannot benefit you economically, you eventually see them not as fellow human beings but as something inferior. It is very ironic that the Europeans migrated to the Americas, Australia, New Zealand and other areas around the world from a background in Europe in which they often faced terrible conditions and issues. Yet, they repeated and far exceeded the injustices and inequalities they received in the new territories they occupied from the indigenous people and the Africans they forced into servitude. Racism corrupts the soul of the culture that practices it.

When different cultures meet and interact with each other, particularly when the distribution of resources is at stake, it is unlikely that all will maintain the consistency of their cultural histories. In the case of the Transatlantic Slave Trade, there were three cultures involved; the European's, Africa's and the indigenous population for an intercultural mix. The Europeans brought in Africans in the Transatlantic Slave Trade to perform free labor in the Americas.

Obviously at that time during the social evolutionary processes of human beings, the Europeans saw this as an opportunity to fundamentally impose their will and culture on the rest of the world. They improved the sophistication and power of the gunpowder-based weapons that they derived from the Chinese. This allowed them to have enormous advantages for fighting wars from a distance. This along with their shipbuilding prowess and development of sea trade routes for commodity markets allowed them to carry out their worldwide mandate.

The Europeans saw an opportunity to develop advanced nations that were constructed upon the principles of political institutions. Everything became mechanized through the introduction of commercial business and industrial sectors. The indigenous people in the conquered, enslaved and colonized countries and continents during the Transatlantic Slave Trade had a simple lifestyle of hunting, fishing and socialization that seemed primitive to the Europeans. The natives didn't have the European's concept of the working wheel nor did they understand how to build roads, buildings, sewerage systems, aqueducts or even work farms.[xxi]

As the Europeans settlers' population grew in the Americas, Africa, Asia and Australia, they simply cleared the indigenous people from tracts of land to make room for themselves and their farms. This disrupted the nomadic life of some of the native tribes and made their survival problematic. Although, some natives, particularly those on the East coast of North America, lived in settled, cities and village. The clearance was deliberate and systematic, resulting in the extinction and genocide of the indigenous people. The tribal cultures of the indigenous American Indians and the Australia Aborigines and others around the world had little chance to succeed when competing with the European settlers in warfare because of their advanced weaponry at that time. The indigenous tribal cultures had little chance to win in an outright competition. [xxii]

Generally, when people deal with someone outside their culture, there is not as strong a feeling to treat them with the same standards as members of their culture. Variables such as race, language and religion, customs, values and beliefs are factors in determining this culture distance and assimilation. During the Transatlantic Slave Trade, the European settlers were not the host society in the territorials around the world they conquered. However, the Europeans considered themselves superior to the indigenous people, so this dysfunction led to not only to a social distance, but an overt antagonism developed between the two racial groups.[xxiii]

When these competing cultures are fixated on the same territories and when there are different concepts making up these cultures, major conflict is inevitable unless there is an agreed cooperation among the cultures. Unless some form of negotiation is clearly understood and implemented by the different cultures, which was not the case, the intent of the Europeans was forced assimilation and control. The indigenous tribal people lost in this cultural competition.

However, an appreciation of one's culture should in no way precludes recognizing that other cultures have value and it should no way preclude treating members of other racial groups with humanity and respect. The European settlers had absolutely no respect for the other world's cultures during that time in world's history except for perhaps the Asians. They also had no interest whatsoever in working with the other world's cultures other than using brute force to conquer, divide, control and destroy. Fortunately, all societies on this earth now do not have the same degree of racists or prejudice people within their ranks. All cultures and societies are not as extreme as others in overcoming race relations. Even within various countries and societies, racist attitudes are not as prevalent in all the parts and regions.

In the United States during the 1830s and 1840s, Manifest Destiny was a widely held belief and concept that called for the country to expand westward toward the Pacific Ocean and conquer the entire territory. They believe it was divine and their God-given right and duty to justify their invasion of the territory from the indigenous people. It was heavily promoted in newspapers, posters and other media. It was also another excuse for displacing the indigenous people who had constantly pushed west as development continued in the United States and impose their cultures on the enslaved Africans and the natives. It was a concept but not official government policy that heavily influenced the policies by many United States Presidents and Governors which led to the passage of the Homestead Act, which encouraged western colonization and territorial acquisition.[xxiv]

17

This type of mentality during the fifteenth through nineteenth centuries played a major role in European and American thought that they were divinely ordained to dominate the world. This of course, actually occurred as a result of pressure to follow this assumption. " The westward expansion of the United States from the Atlantic Ocean to the Pacific Ocean included the Treaty of Paris (1783) involving the 13 colonies; the Louisiana Purchase (1803) involving fifteen U.S. states; the Florida (Spanish) Cession (1819) involving Florida, parts of Alabama, Mississippi, and Louisiana; the Texas Annexation (1845); the Oregon Territory (1846) involving Oregon, Washington, Idaho and parts of Wyoming and Montana; the Mexican Cession (1848) involving all or parts of California, Nevada, Arizona, Colorado, New Mexico, Utah and Wyoming; and the Gadsden Purchase (1853)" [xxv] involving the southern part of New Mexico allowed the United States to expand its territory throughout the entire North American continent except Mexico.

The end result was that the destiny became true much to the detriment of indigenous people in those territorials and other cultures around the world. The Manifest Destiny concept had some internal limitations because some people opposed the expansion of the institution of slavery in some of the territories.

During the existing world racial order which started in the fifteenth-century, the history of the enslaved Africans to the Americas and the Caribbean, the Europeans' forced entry into Africa, the Americas, Asia, Australia and New Zealand to colonize most of the world involved an organized calculated network of intertwined racial issues that were designed to keep people of color and the raw materials in the territorials that they resided under their control. Africans were brought there against their will to supply free labor to build territories in the Americas and the Caribbean. The European settlers sadistically eradicated the indigenous people in the Americas, Africa, Asia, Australia and

New Zealand into oblivion and fundamentally imposed their will on the rest of the world.

The decision made by the European powers to conquer the world was done in the most brutal inhumane conditions imaginable whose legacy and challenges will still be felt in the next few decades and centuries. The facts associated with this matter are vast and deep with an astoundingly long deep-rooted history. The history of global racism in our culture is abhorrent; the wounds are deep. It took centuries to create this global wide racial system and it will take decades or even centuries to dismantle it. The European powers created a legacy of racism and discrimination that warped almost every aspect of global life and politics that continues today. They disrupted lives and global communities, causing long-term trauma that continues to reverberate. The savage nature of the Transatlantic Slave Trade led to the destruction of entire cultures. Unfortunately, there are no quick fixes or one fit solution.

The dominant culture is firmly entrenched in virtually all of world's social institutional structures and systems. The dominant culture created these very complex global societal problems. It presently has complete control of all the world's major institutional and systems. Some members of the dominant culture are trying to preserve a global wide social racial hierarchy that was created by their ancestors in the fifteenth century that didn't have a practical reason to even exist except to dominate other human beings and feel intrinsically superior to members of other racial groups because of their genetic makeups and lineage and their cultures. They will have to play a major role in executing global strategies to change or reform them.

There is only one race and it is the human race. During the twenty-first century, members of the subordinate groups are still living at the crossroads of some very trying racial global issues. Ideally all members of the human race must do their part to build mutually inclusive global societies that respect everyone and reject racism, prejudice, biases, hatred and discrimination based on based solely on an attribute of a person's genetic makeup and lineage that someone cannot change. For this to happen, the global racial order which was created in the fifteenth century must be completely dismantled.

The struggle and quest for global racial justice must commence and continue with the full knowledge of how the racial divides were socially manufactured and politically sustained before we can learn how to overcome them. The full acknowledgment of the sordid history of racism in the North America, South America, Africa, Australia, Asia and Europe is the first step towards dismantling it. No postmodern or poststructuralist dismantling of race can disregard the sustained history of global racism as presently constructed and the institutions and systems that maintain it.[xxvi] We must acknowledge the truth and beauty of our global history as well as the selfishness and injustice of our ancestors. This acknowledgement will allow us to wrestle with a complex past to help us write a different storyline for the future.[xxvii] In order to overcome global racism, it must first be acknowledged.

SYSTEMIC GLOBAL RACISM PRINCIPLES

The underlying principles of systemic institutional racism must be understood so that people impacted will know how to deal with them. Many of these racial inequality issues still affect most of the members of the subordinate groups to this very day. Each principle will be considered below.

THE DOMINANT CULTURE DOES NOT SHARE POWER WITH OTHER RACIAL GROUPS

Racism is a system that ensures an unequal distribution of resources between racial groups. Because the dominant culture dominates all significant global institutions, their interests and priorities are fully embedded in the foundation of the global society. So, the system of unequal institutional racial power is fundamental to understanding group power relationships. Individuals from one of other subordinate racial groups can sit at the tables of power, but most decision-makers will be from the dominant culture.

Racism is also a deeply-rooted system around the globe that disadvantages and devalues people of color as a group and advantages and empowers lighter skin people as a group, regardless of whether those individuals wish to be advantaged or empowered in that way.

The dominant culture presently has built in advantages and institutional privileges over people of darker color. That is why that in every category of people's activities worldwide from health care, education, economic, criminal justice system, entertainment, labor, law, politics, religion, sex and war, people of color as a class live in inferior position as compared to people with lighter skin tones. Presently, there has little credence or acceptance for lessening these advantages, benefits, favors and privileges.

21

IT IS SET UP FOR THE GROUP AND NOT THE INDIVIDUAL

Generally, people operating out of self-interest do not surrender their privileges, freedoms and heritages unless they are persuaded there is something better ahead. Many members of the dominant group regularly vote against their own best interest to protect their tribe or group and the status quo.

Racism is not ascribed to an entire racial group but a characteristic of individuals within it. Membership in a dominant or subordinate group is generally not voluntary although the various European nationalities were able to successfully assimilate into the American dominant culture. People are generally born into the group. Thus, race, gender, ethnicity and religion are considered ascribed statuses.[xxviii] Racism disregards the actual source of an individual's character and replaces it with physiologically determined traits, completely out of that individual's control. It ascribes moral and social significance to that which, in fact, based solely on attributes of a person's genetic makeup and lineage, which is of no consequence.

Racism is the practice of judging individual character or social standing according to one's racial group. It judges individuals by their membership in their group rather than by their own ideas and actions. While individual whites may be against racism, they still benefit from the distribution of resources controlled by their group.

Generally, when a deplorable crime happens, and the suspect is a member of the dominant culture, he is individualized based on his racial group. The overriding racial narrative is they were 'bad apples' or had mental problems and there is not a judgment of the actions of one member of the dominant culture against the entire racial group. Even if the victim of the crime is a member of the subordinate group, his character is usually criminalized to

22

minimize the crime. If, on the other hand, the suspect is a member of the subordinate groups, an entire racial group is demonized for the actions of one person. They are perceived as dangerous, threatening, unruly, uncivilized, thugs, gangster and part of a bad culture.

Results matter for everyone except when the dominant culture assesses how members of the subordinate group perform in their chosen field of endeavor. A different metric may apply If you are a high performer. The dominant culture will say that you are just special, one of the 'good ones', or an anomaly and not the norm for your group. The rest of the members in your subordinate group are the norm. Likewise, if you have a misstep, they will blame your entire group or tribe for the misdeed. Members of your subordinate group are not allowed to be individuals like other groups. They are expected to represent their group. No matter how intelligent, wealthy or possess elite upbringings, a member of the subordinate group may be, the dominant culture does not see them as a part of their culture. They are still a member of the subordinate group culture. That means a subordinate group member can never just be his own person. There is an assumption made that all subordinate group members think alike and share similar views. On the other hand, dominant group members can speak on any particular subject without being the sole representative for their entire racial group.

No person should have to carry the burden of their racial group on their shoulders. Racial groups at the top of society's racial social order don't have this burden and neither should subordinate group members. This is very unfair, and this type of mindset needs to change.

IT IS PROPAGANDISTIC

Media have tremendous power in shaping global racial discourse. A very common and pervasive mindset throughout human history is that just about anything can be justified and interpreted to justify man's intents.

The shrewdness of the dominant culture's agenda and propaganda have caused some of its gullible dominate group members to fall prey for its message and allow some gullible members of the subordinate groups to swallow in despair from centuries of abuses. Some members of the dominant group were so intricate in their indoctrination and brainwashing of racism that they managed to plant seeds of self-hatred, unworthiness and degradation into the minds of the subordinate group members. The seeds would grow and create hatred for subordinate group members by their other group members thereby destroying the spirit of the entire group. This has led to a lack of self-esteem among some subordinate group members who have a poor perception of themselves. They sometime take out their frustrations on other subordinate group members who look like them and live in close proximity with each other. They feel their lives are devalued and some resort to anti-social behaviors, thus fulfilling a self-fulfilling prophecy propagated by racist myths.

The propaganda machine by the dominant culture over the past five centuries during the existing world order on other subordinate racial groups to justify its top status has been craftily developed. It has questioned the intellect of those on the lower echelon end of society's racial social order by setting standards that they cannot reach, and they are never clued on. Public policy decisions were made to keep the African American's unemployment numbers twice the rate for the dominant culture, their children were sent to segregated schools that received less property tax funding and housing policies and were designed to keep them in the inner city through redlining. The long history of slavery, Apartheid, oppression, and segregation are rarely mentioned by the dominant culture.

In essence, as subordinate group members, many are set up for failure. They are then blame for not 'pulling themselves up by their bootstraps' and described as always being overly emotional and angry. Being angry is a natural response for being systematically oppressed. They find themselves constantly defending and proving themselves, their full complex humanity, their right to life and who they are. Therefore, nothing really gets done and their realities become a vicious cycle.

In most global pluralistic societies, subordinate group members have always had to prove themselves. It has been that way since the beginning of the Transatlantic Slave Trade. African Americans in particular have had to constantly prove that they were part of the fabric of that society and the building of the country they resided in. Thus, they had to earn themselves into positions of leadership and responsibilities until they were respected and considered as equals. Sometimes, even after obtaining those hard-earned positions, some dominant culture members are still skeptical of their abilities.

The history of nations through textbooks are written by the dominant culture who has a vested interest in how the story was and is being told. Throughout the history of humankind, the victor rewrites the history books. In most cases, the untruths are told. For example, some history textbooks distributed to public schools in the United States describe slaves as unpaid interns. In another example, fourth graders in a school district were asked by their teacher in a school assignment to give three good reasons for slavery and three bad reasons. Although assignments on many subjects are designed to spark a debate, no one should be required to understand the merits of slavery that is based on hatred, inferiority, bigotry and racism. It further illustrates the insensitivity that some members of the dominant group possess and the racial inequalities that still exist.[xxix]

Some gullible members of the dominant culture are not well versed of the issues in their societies. They have been given false racial narratives of their portrayal of subordinate group members around the world that have a different skin tone from them. For example, Arabs are terrorists, Islam is a bad religion, African Americans are gangster and live on welfare, Hispanics as illegal immigrants, welfare recipients, less educated and refuse to learn English, Native Americans as alcohol abusers, Asian Americans as being perpetual foreigners despite born in the country, etc. On the other hand, the racial narrative of members of the dominant culture are described as honest, hard-working, disciplined, rigorous, successful and rugged individuals.

The popular dominant culture created these inaccurate and negative representation of subordinate racial groups comprised by unreliable stereotypes. They are harmful to the group in that these images consist of unpleasant and awkward imagery based on assumptions created by racist myths that have a causal effect on people's perceptions. The media portrayal of the subordinate groups does them a great disservice that is misleading the public. These negative stereotypes have been perpetuated and ingrained so much in some societies that some people believe them to be facts.

They give this false notion that subordinate racial groups are the cause of all their social ills and everything wrong with the world. It never mentions the overwhelming number of people of color who are very productive citizens. It just dwells on the negativity of a few members of the subordinate groups who commits crime over and over on the news. It rarely blames the dominant culture for its actions.

26

The dominant culture is in control of media mogul institutions that make these decisions. Their unwittingly victims either don't know or care to know what is happening and don't get the true picture of positive things happening in the marginalized communities. The information they received is not analyzed or vetted so they go on with their lives as though the subordinate group members of society's racial social order are responsible for all the problems of the world.

Also, some members of the dominant culture are just caught in a system which benefits them indirectly because of their skin color. They then feel compelled to defend the system. Propaganda has been instrumental and played a key role in their actions. This has created some bitterness and resentment by the subordinate group members who has been victimized for centuries by the legacy of oppression and global racism.

IT IS RUTHLESS, UNJUST AND DISREGARDS A PERSON'S MORAL CODE

Global racism is a moral issue because it involves how we treat our fellow human beings. When acts of racism occur, it not only harms the social standards of those persons and their racial groups but their freedom, independence and well-being as well. Any society concerned with combating racism within its ranks should also be interesting in promoting certain dispositions among its members treating them with tolerance, decency, respect and fairness. xxx In the case of the Transatlantic Slave Trade and the genocide of the indigenous people world-wide, the danger of defining groups of people as inferior is that one no longer feels morally obligated to treat them as human beings.

There is an undergoing debate as to whether a global moral code exist among all the world's societies. There is a belief that there is an innate global moral code that exist in every society. This is based on the premise that there are inherent understandings of what is morally right and wrong among most human beings. But based on cultural differences we may apply the code differently; the universal moral code remains the same. Throughout our lives we have conditioned ourselves to either stray from this moral code or abide by it. As individuals and societies grow, they may become defiant to the moral code. But because this is at odds with their nature, they attempt to justify their actions through various means in order to condition their opposition of the global moral code.

Then there is an opposite belief that there is no universal moral code. Instead, morality is determined by the standards of the members within the cultures and societies. Moral standards also changed or improved over a time period within the same culture in which their descendants understood aspects of morality better than those of earlier times. For example, slavery, Jim Crow laws, and Black Codes were legal and considered moral in many parts of the Americas during the Transatlantic Slave Trade that ended in the late 1880's. However, this ideology changed during subsequent generations after being challenged internally or by other cultures and societies. People's beliefs, values and ideas are constantly changing and evolving. What was labeled as wrong a few decades or centuries ago, is accepted today. Likewise, what is labeled as wrong or right today, may probably be accepted or rejected in the near future.

Every culture and sub-culture have different social standards and belief system in what is accepted as moral. This was formed by their history and the current society. Although in modern society, because the world is 'shrinking' due to technology and becoming more diverse due to immigration patterns, it is lessening. As a result, what is considered wrong and right has become more or less accepted throughout the world. The differences in the moral code for human beings was more apparent when the world was not as interdependent as it is today. This is a belief that the moral code of a society is affected by many factors including its culture, current leadership, non-monolith or monolith society, geography, history and others.

IT IS DECEPTIVE, CUNNING AND EVASIVE

The framework of systemic racism is the same. It just keeps getting dressed differently over a period of time to maintain its effectiveness. The decision makers in some political jurisdictions have learned to say abstracts things and use coded language such as state's rights, inner city, forced busing, law and order, illegal alien, Shariah law, welfare and food stamps, nationality and tax cuts when talking about racial issues. They have learned to tone down their rhetoric with respectability over the years and at the same time still mean the same thing.

Outspokenness and public acts and display of racism are no longer prevalent in most societies as they were in the past. Over time, racism has transformed from a blatant and overt form into a passive style of prejudice and discrimination. Today's racism is stealthy and unspoken, and often deftly covered up with fabricated cover stories to legitimize the inequalities. "Obvious displays of racism still occur, and they are quickly decried. But these days racism has mostly gone underground; no longer in your face, racial discrimination hides, embedded in institutions and systems of oppression, difficult for the average person to pinpoint.[xxxi]

Nowadays, it is often used as a means to express frustration or opinions on obvious differences about another racial group in a way that is not obvious enough to be noticeable. This new breed of racism is perhaps more difficult to fight against its more egregious past. Its subtlety allows its perpetuators to claim ignorance of any racism, and its lack of media attentions lulls fellow citizens into complacence and acceptance of the current system. Furthermore, many people are unaware of their racist behaviors as it has become so deep seated within our society. As a result, the acts of subtle racism are often mistaken as normal and acceptable behavior.

Racism does not depend on lighter skinned tone people to do its work. Sometimes subordinate member's hands are tied by the very law they took an oath of allegiance to pledge. Likewise, in the beginning, many racial group members have an honorable intention to make a difference or try to change the system internally. However, the system is so entrenched in its culture that the person may have good intentions at first to change it and make a difference. But because of its complexities, he becomes a victim of it and is engulfed by it.

Some subordinate group members have fallen for the dominant culture's agenda and propaganda and just swallow in despair from centuries of abuses. Sometimes when subordinate group members are mentally and spiritually infected with the dominant culture, they will act in servitude of it and contrary to their own social economic survival and interest. Their socialization and livelihood demand it.

It seems that unless someone from the dominant group culture voices concerns and issues with the plight of the subordinate groups, it doesn't carry much weight. No matter how much this has been said, stated, spoken by the subordinate group member, it only becomes legitimate when someone who is not a member of the subordinate group speaks it. Members of the subordinate groups have been saying the same things for years, but it takes a member of the dominant group to validate it before it is fully acknowledged. On the other hand, when the denial strategy has run its course and is a losing strategy, then someone from the dominant group must grudgingly and painfully validate the messages.

The conquerors and dominant cultures define the law to fit their agenda. For example, slavery, Apartheid, Jim Crows laws and Black Codes were legal by government entities in the United States and South Africa. It took a revolutionary Civil War, a Civil Rights movement, and internal and foreign pushback from citizens, countries and groups to change the laws. Also, in the 1980's in the United States, there was a crack cocaine epidemic in the black communities in many cities around America that became a national crisis. Many blacks were imprisoned because of drug usage. In the 2010's, there is an opioid epidemic that is primarily in the white communities. Now, instead of seeking incarceration for the opioid users as was the case with crack cocaine users, public policy makers and politicians advocated counseling and treatment centers. So, race base policies occur all the time and selective enforcement is generally used. A more humane approach was taken for white victims, yet it had devastating effect on the crack cocaine users as well as their communities.

Also, the dominant culture has a history of pitting one subordinate group against the other subordinate groups, so the dominant group can maintain its power. Historically, due to some deep hostilities between these subordinate groups in which the seeds were sowed by the dominant group, it has kept the subordinate groups from uniting in a common cause against the inequalities of the dominant group. Examples include prejudicial views by some members of African descent against LGBT members. There has been some mounting tensions and hostilities between the Asians and African communities involving Korean American's shop owners, overrepresentation at universities and the 'model minority' vs. 'bad minority' stereotyping concept. There have also been some strained relationships between some African Americans and Hispanics in issues such as skin-color prejudices, societal socioeconomic ladder preferences, spike in criminal violence and illegal immigration status among others.

As a result, there are few ties between the subordinate groups and they even discriminate against each other. Around the world, subordinate groups have an evolving relationship. Separately, they have faced economic, social, political and cultural disadvantages and have more in common than ever before. It remains to be seen if they will eventually form a collaboration and deal with these hardships together.

IT IS NARCISSISTIC

Some members in the dominant groups are such under evolved individuals. They literally have no culture, hold on to accomplishments of people that looked like them and claim it as their own. They are under accomplished and have no substance of who they are or what they are, so they claim they did everything great in life and try to take away from other subordinate racial groups. It has a narcissistic outlook where they come from a background of being held to high esteem yet fail to meet their own standards and deal with their own insecurities and realities. So, they try to bring others down to make themselves feel better because there is nothing else from within.

It is oddly presumptive that someone who has never experienced the ill effects of racism, discrimination or disparate treatment can feel so empowered to tell someone who has, that it's time to get over it all the while ignoring the fact of such behaviors and the damage it has caused and continues today. Imagine how exhausting and burdensome it is for a member of the subordinate group to directly contend with racism every day for decades.

IT IS HISTORICAL

The dominant culture never takes responsibility for problems they started in history. Some also think that can escape history. It refuses to face the truth about the very unpleasant parts of its history. It has become a politically correct spin on historical events to denigrate the acts of the Europeans and Americans and point to the wrongdoings and missteps of the subordinate groups. This is clearly a misuse of history. They live for the present, the status quo and hold on to long established traditions and customs.

There is also a selective memory on historical facts. Every nation has a creation myth, or origin myth, which is the story people are taught of how the nation came into being. For example, the United States began with Columbus' so-called "discovery" of America, continued with settlement by brave Pilgrims, won its independence from England with the American Revolution, and then expanded westward until it became the enormous, rich country you see today.[xxxii] That is the origin myth. It omits the key facts about the birth and growth of the United States as a nation with the genocide of the indigenous people and the enslavement of the African people during the Transatlantic Slave Trade routes. Those facts demonstrate that racism is fundamental to the existence of the country.

IT IS PSEUDO-SCIENTIFIC

Propaganda often has pseudo-science to make claims about the superiority of one racial group over other racial groups. Eugenics based on this pseudoscience was one of the atrocities that occurred against indigenous people and Africans during the Transatlantic Slave Trade in the fifteen century and against Jews by the Germans during WWII in concentration camps and even illegal immigration and other atrocities around the world.

Pseudo-science is a claim that is presented as scientific but lacking any supporting evidence, cannot be tested and those not adhere to a valid scientific method. However, it should be noted that there is no such thing as 'absolute truth' in science. Every proposal is just a theory which stands if evidence supports it. This is one of the loopholes that proponents of pseudo-science use to make their arguments sound convincing so technically they don't have to prove anything absolutely.

Pseudo-science is something that appears to be scientific but is not based on real facts. When the facts are vetted and studied, pseudo-science moves closer towards myths than facts and truths. Because of propaganda, many people still look at pseudoscience as an excuse to express their hatred, bigotry, racism and prejudice toward other individuals and racial groups. The so-called scientific theories about race have largely been discredit in its ordinary usage today. Although it has been invalidated many times over, some form of this ideology still persists today.

IT IS MILITARISTIC

The militaristic racism of policing is deployed in several countries around the world including Israel, South Africa and the United States. The policing of violence against members of subordinate group members in a militaristic context has been used extensively in many racial events and incidents. In the United States, in recent decades, many law enforcement agencies around the country are equipped with surplus military supplies and equipment. During the Civil Rights era, the National Guard units were routinely called upon to quell racial violence and tensions between racial groups in several cities throughout the country. This continued after the Civil Rights movement in the war against drugs, terrorist acts and other major criminal activities. When the militarization of policing is used in quell racial violence, while the cultural difference between the dominant and subordinate groups are relevant, political decisions in those jurisdictions and at the highest levels of government are also made. This is/was especially relevant in many Civil Rights incidents and current Israel/Palestinian conflicts where the militarization of policing can reinforce rather than improve ethnic prejudice, racism and discrimination.

During Apartheid, the South African Defense Force (SADF) were used in quelling opposition to minority rule, often supporting the South Africa Police. In addition to its conventional military responsibilities, it was organized to counter possible insurgency in all forms.

The United States is a nation state created by military conquest in several stages. The first stage was the European seizure of the lands inhabited by indigenous peoples, which they called Turtle Island, the original name for North America. Turtle Island was renamed North America and South America after Spanish explorer, Amerigo Vespucci. That process must be called genocide, and it created the land base of this country. The elimination of indigenous peoples and seizure of their land was the first condition for its existence.[xxxiii]

PART TWO - WORLD ORDER FORMATION

Global racism did not begin five centuries ago during the existing racial world order when several European countries set out to colonize, enslave and conquer the world. Racism roots crosses ages, cultures, racial groups, religions, centuries and millennia. The trade in human slaves goes back as far as human's first civilizations. The ancient civilizations had slaves and the practice was common throughout the known world of that time. Slavery in ancient cultures was known to occur in civilizations as old as Sumer, and it was found in every civilization, including Ancient Egypt, the Akkadian Empire, Assyria, Ancient Greece, Rome Empire, Hebrew kingdoms, Ancient China, Ancient India, and Ancient levant.[xxxiv]

Although the Transatlantic Slave Trade was the largest and most well-known, there were many more. The first mention of slavery belongs in the Mesopotamian Code of Hammurabi during the period 3500 BC – 500 BC. It is estimated that at the turn of the nineteenth century, three quarters of the world was enslaved or in bondage. One of the largest scale trades was the Arabs in the western Africa to the Arabian Peninsula.

In Africa during ancient times, its earliest civilizations or societies (groups of people) were the beginning of the first world orders. Scientists through DNA research testing on African mummies, historians and anthropological records disclosed and documented the presence of Egyptian and West African culture and African presence all over the planet. Later, when many Africans migrated and practiced vagility around the world, this led to the later development and foundation in Europe, Asia, Americas and Australia and other places around the world. Millennia later, the builders of the Egypt pyramids show a mathematics and physics formulas still yet unknown. Since the rise of the Abrahamic religions and the Roman Empire, Africans' land was pillaged, the people were murdered, raped, massacred, demoralized and technologically deprived by subsequent European world orders.

Even China's dynasties have come and gone, and much of their ancient and mythical culture and heritage have been lost. China was once known as the Land of the Divine. Legend has it that each dynasty came from a unique paradise. Over the course of five millennia, emperors, heroes, sages, and generals used their wisdom and virtue to lay the groundwork for China's rich culture. Decades of communist suppression had left the culture scarred and impoverished. But some Chinese have been united on a mission to revive their cultural heritage and share it with the world.[xxxv]

There has been a lot of debate as to the first recorded civilizations or societies as well as the continuous ones that are still recognizable today. They include the Egyptians, Ethiopians, China, Japan, Persians, Indus Valley, Romans, Mesopotamian, Aztecs, Mayans, Incas and others that are between 2,000 to 5,000 years. "Curator Hamady Bocoum told the Associated Press that proof of African civilization is at least 7,000 years old, referencing a skull discovered in present-day Chad."[xxxvi] The definition of a civilization or empire may not be the same as modern day nations and may not be prominent political entities. Today, civilizations and empires are referred to as societies. Some of these civilizations or societies have survived over time but may be less recognizable and prominent since their peak periods. Many have evolved over time and continue to exist to this day in some form. Many historians consider Mesopotamia and Egypt as the two oldest ones that developed in the region where southwest Asia joins northwest Africa.

The victors write the history books, so Africa's story is largely untold. Africa's history and the memory of its history disciplines of study have not been erased, reprogrammed and replaced by the conquering dominant cultures. Many African nations had royalties, palaces and extensive civilizations or societies. African history, except for the parts about recent Colonization is never taught in any schools except in Africa. The problem is that the history of Africa is not as well studied or taught in many other areas of the world. That has led to a great deal of misinformation and ignorance about many of Africa's ancient societies and regions. It is incumbent upon African historians to promote Africa history to the West to dispel these racist myths. Likewise, Africa needs to adopt the same mindset as China in reviving its cultural heritages. Otherwise, you risk being defined by other cultures around the world which is now the case. Africa needs to revive its cultural heritage and share it with the world. This education will perpetrate the stereotype that Africans have done nothing but become colonized, enslaved, poor, and in tribal wars.

There is undeniable and compelling evidence concurred by historians, anthropologists, and archeologists of the massive looting by Europe and America of Africa artifacts dating back to ancient times, slavery era, colonialism and the present imperialistic era. "The looting of a country's resources is a common trait with the European colonizers. They pillage and take everything of value to enrich their own nations, this is not any different with valuable parts of a country's history. There is always talk about the many vaults filled with gold, diamonds, and platinum from Africa, but there are galleries filled with ancient African history, relics, sculpture spoils from a bitter past.

There is growing interest from the pillaged nations for the return of these artworks to their home nation. Original pieces of significant importance in the continent's heritage, artwork from the home nation's skilled craftsmen and women.

Many of these artworks are gathering dust at many foreign museums, you see statues from Egypt, which clearly resemble the facial features of black Africans displayed at the British Museums.

Art imitates life and knowing more about how their ancestors as Africans lived is imperative for future generations. It connects the African continent to the fabric of our history. Depriving the youth of Africa their true history is equally deceptive as it is unjust.

There have been calls to return the artifacts to their native lands to no avail. In a recent chain of events Benin, a former French colony, requested their artifacts be returned to the country of origin. These works were looted by the French government. This is everything from stones, chains, jewels artwork, objects that have been in France for over a century."xxxvii

A new Museum of Black Civilizations that was decades in the making opened in Dakar, Senegal in December 2018 amid a global conversation about the ownership and legacy of African art. "It was the realization of Leopold Sedar Senghor, Senegal's first President, vision to create a museum that would represent the histories and contemporary cultures of Black people everywhere."xxxviii The nation's culture Minister of the West African nation wants the thousands of pieces of cherished heritages taken from the continent during the recent centuries of European colonization, turmoil and rule returned. The 148,00 square foot circular structure is one of the largest of its kind in Africa. It is complicated by the fact that countless of artifacts have been dispersed around the world by the undeniable crimes of European colonization. Pressure is being mounted on museums outside Africa to return art and artifacts plundered during the Colonial era. Therefore, the museum will not have a permanent collection until the African nation obtains their legacy objects.

Exhibitions in the museum will include 50 pieces on loan from France and more than 5000 pieces of Senegalese objects were identified as coming from Senegal alone. A report commissioned by the French President Emmanuel Macron recommended that the French give back works taken without consent. The French President also pledged to return 26 pieces to Benin and is just one of many countries loaning works to the new museum. The museum and other nations will start negotiations with other countries to for a return of those objects. The museum, with its focus on Africa and the diaspora will highlight the continent as the 'cradle of civilization'. It is working with dozens of institutions around the world to plan future exhibitions. For so long, the artistic history of an entire continent has largely been told by others or stowed away in faraway museums. This new museum will be a forced recognition of how much Africans brought to the world and hoping to change the narrative. Africa is the cradle of humankind. The artworks and artifacts were taken from the continent of Africa, but it plans to reclaim them in the future.[xxxix]

Meanwhile, also in December 2018, the European country of Belgium unveiled a restored $84 million makeover of 119,000 square feet of its Africa Museum that is often branded as the 'last Colonial museum'. The museum had previously promoted the former Belgian King Leopold II's imperial venture into the Congo that included an exhibition of war booty that included a human zoo. Now much of its original content stands in homage but the museum has undergone a major renovation to 'decolonize' it prestigious but highly controversial collection. In the past, the museum had presented a positive view of its Colonial legacy.

The museum director admitted that at least 80 percent of African art is currently found in Europe and that Africa had a right to retain control over its own cultural history. The museum says it will consider claims for restitution if and when they are officially made. He said that a major urgency is for the reintroduction of Belgium's Colonial past in the Congo into education. The controversial subject has been disappearing from many schools and the young children did not know anything about their countries' involvement in the Congo.[xl]

"The list of things that the European colonizers took away from Africa is endless. One priceless piece of our identity that was wickedly snatched from Africa is their artifacts that are now scattered all over the world, miles away from their native lands. Africa's desperate calls for the return of these objects of cultural heritage have largely been met with disdain and unabashed defense of the indefensible.

The British are the biggest culprits of the shameful plunder of Africa's cultural treasures, with the country's museums having become a trove of stolen works of art. To the looters, African's artifacts hold nothing more than aesthetic and monetary value, but to Africa, the pieces carry their history, cultures, and their very sense of being and identity. These works of art timelessly document the history of families, clans, and villages that made up ancient African societies. With most of that indigenous knowledge having been erased and stolen from us, they are left with little evidence of Africa's pre-colonial history.

In 1897, the British invaded the Benin Empire, a pre-colonial nation that was located in what is now Southern Nigeria. Troops ruthlessly burnt the empire to the ground, killing thousands and wiping out one of the richest cultures of ancient Africa. The king was forced to flee while his palace was looted of its treasures such as the bronze and ivory artefacts that chronicled the history and customs of the kingdom. Commonly described as the Benin Bronzes, these plaques and sculptures were numbered in the thousands and ended up in European and American museums.

Two of the famous Benin Bronzes, the Ahianwen-Oro artwork, were returned to their homeland in 2014 by British citizen, Dr. Mark Walker, leading to calls for repatriation of more artifacts. Walker had inherited the artwork from his great-grandfather, who took part in the pillaging of Benin.

Many of the known Benin Bronzes remain at the British Museum, where they are still on display. Nigeria has repeatedly requested for the return of its cultural heritage, but the British Museum won't budge.

Egypt has been consistently campaigning for Germany to return the statue of Queen Nefertiti. The Germans took the 3,400-year-old bust of the great queen in 1913 using fraudulent documents. The country reportedly considered returning the statue in 1935, but Hitler decided against it.

While Egyptians struggle to get what is rightfully theirs, Germany continues to profit from Nefertiti. The figure draws more than a million visitors every year to the Neues Museum in Berlin, which explains why the European country keeps monopolizing the artwork.

Egypt has also been pushing to get back the Rosetta Stone, the 2,200-year-old slab of black basalt with a hieroglyphic, demotic and Greek inscription that was the linguistic key to deciphering Egyptian hieroglyphics. The stone was shipped out of the North African country in 1799 during French colonial rule and is now in possession of the British Museum. It's unclear how it ended in the hands of the British, but what is certain is that there was no consent from the Egyptians.

In 1868, the British captured Magdala, Emperor Tewodros II's mountain capital in Northwest Ethiopia, and left destruction in their wake. Among other crimes, the British Army looted Ethiopian churches of a range of valuable cultural objects and treasures, including crowns, gold and silver crosses, and numerous manuscripts documenting Ethiopia's history from the era of Solomon and Sheba to the early 19th century. Various illustrated Ge'ez manuscripts were also stolen.

According to historian, Richard Pankhurst, who campaigned tirelessly for the return of Ethiopian cultural artefacts, more than ten elephants were needed to carry the plunder across the Bashilo

River to the nearby Dalanta Plain. Some of the artefacts were auctioned off while others are still held at the British Museum, Victoria and Albert Museum, and the Queen's Library at Windsor Castle.

Many other treasures were stolen from Ethiopia. In 2005, Italy returned an ancient granite obelisk almost seven decades after it was plundered by Italian troops.

When Europeans "discovered" the Great Zimbabwe Kingdom in the 16th century, they refused to believe that Native Africans built such a civilization. The Great Zimbabwe Monument was constructed between the 11th and 14th centuries by the indigenous Shona People, and it serves as a testament to ancient African civilization that existed before colonization.

Found in the monument were a series of cultural artefacts, including soapstone bird carvings known as the Zimbabwe Bird. Needless to say, these artworks were pillaged and sent to museums across Europe and America.

Colonizer, Cecil John Rhodes, took some of the stone-carved birds to South Africa, four of which were returned in 1981, a year after Zimbabwe gained independence. A part of one of the birds ended up in the hands of a German missionary, who sold it to the Ethnological Museum in Berlin in 1907. The museum finally handed back the piece to Zimbabwe in 2003.

Once known as the world's most expensive piece of African art, the Bangwa Queen has exchanged hands of many art collectors since she was stolen from her royal shrine in Cameroon. The wooden sculpture, which is believed to be more than a thousand years old, was taken away by German colonial explorer, Gustav Conrau, in the 1890s.

Conrau entered the Bangwa Village under the guise of seeking trade relations and supplies, only to snatch the memorial statue right under the owner's nose. In 1990, the artwork sold at a New

York auction for a record-breaking $3.4 million, making it the world's most expensively priced African artwork at the time."[xli]

In addition, after the release of the groundbreaking report by the French government calling for the restitution of Colonial artifacts to African countries, including the Ivory Coast, Nigeria and other sub-Saharan parts of Africa. In total, France occupied or colonized, at various times, at least 20 current or former countries in Africa. The full report mentions that France's holdings of cultural objects from its Colonial empire are vast and include objects from Africa, Asia, Oceania and the Americas. A major concern is that the French museums could 'emptied' and duplicates or facsimiles of objects, where appropriate, was recommended.[xlii]

Many Europeans thought that Africa's history was not important. They argued that Africans were inferior to Europeans and they used this to help justify slavery and Apartheid. However, the reality was very different. A study of African history shows that Africa was by no means inferior to Europe. As you can see below, the people who suffered the most from the Transatlantic Slave Trade were civilized, organized and technologically advanced peoples, long before the arrival of European slavers, trying to suggest they were backward peoples. [xliii] Once the real history is revealed to the world, Africans stands just as high as other racial groups in contributing to the progress of the world.

Africans had plenty of significant and great civilizations or societies. Despite there being debates about it, many people believe that ancient Egyptians were blacks who descended from East Africans and historians have evidence that support this belief. A few examples include the Zulus, who held their own against both the Dutch and British; the Malian Empire, Carthage, Sheba, Sudan, Ghana, Benin Empire, Ashanti Kingdom, Maravi Kingdom, Songhai Empire, the Merina Kingdom. A big part of

Africa's history is the country of Ethiopia. It is one of the few countries in the world never to have been colonized or invaded by the Europeans and it once occupied Egypt for centuries.

Egypt was the first of many great African civilizations. It lasted thousands of years and achieved many magnificent and incredible things in the fields of science, mathematics, medicine, technology and the arts. Egyptian civilization was already over 2000 years old by the time the city of Rome was built. [xliv] Few Ancient African civilizations have been studied as extensively. One that certainly has is Ancient Egypt. Considering the degree of their advancement and the age within which they developed (usually starting around 2650-2500 BC for Egypt compared to Ancient Rome's projected 750 BC start).

The Aksumites (present day Ethiopia/Eritrea) had a significant trade and military hegemony over the Red Sea area starting from around the 1st century AD. They even invaded the South Arabian region (present day Yemen) and established a port colony. They minted their own coins. Their erected gigantic Obelisks and Palaces that are still being excavated. They are part of some mythologies involving the Queen of Sheba and there are even some who believe that the Arc of the Covenant went there after the destruction of the Temple of Jerusalem which is debatable and unproven. They were in contact with the Byzantine Empire in the fifth and sixth centuries. There is even a documented military alliance between Emperor Justinian and King Kaleb of Aksum in South Arabia.[xlv]

Sudan/Nubia built an Egyptian influence society that even at one-point conquered Egypt (the 25th Dynasty). There is extensive knowledge on the Ancient Kingdoms of ancient Sudan. It was a well-known civilization whose history is intertwined with its neighboring nation, Egypt. Aksum was a major Christian power, an ally of the Byzantines that conquered some South Arabian states like Himyar at the height of their power and laid the foundation for the unique history of Ethiopia.

There was a Ghana empire, though not located in present day Ghana. It was replaced by the Mali Empire, which was famous for its wealth and learning. Eastern Senegal and Ghana made up the Empire of Ghana which was ruled by a king. In the west of Africa, the kingdom of Ghana was a vast Empire that spread across an area the size of Western Europe. Between the ninth and thirteenth centuries, it traded in gold, salt and copper. It was like a medieval European empire, with a collection of powerful local rulers, controlled by one king or emperor. Ghana was highly advanced and prosperous. It is said that the Ghanaian ruler had an army of 200,000 men.[xlvi] One king of the Empire of Ghana was kind to foreigners. He provided the majority of the knowledge of the Empire of Ghana.

The kingdoms of Benin and Ife were led by the Yoruba people and sprang up between the 11th and 12th centuries. The Ife civilization goes back as far as 500BC and its people made objects from bronze, brass, copper, wood and ivory. Studies of the Benin show that they were highly skilled in ivory carving, pottery, rope and gum production.

From the thirteenth to the fifteenth century, the kingdom of Mali spread across much of West and North-East Africa. At its largest, the kingdom was 2000 kilometers wide and there was an organized trading system, with gold dust and agricultural produce being exported north. Mali reached its height in the 14th century. Cowrie shells were used as a form of currency and gold, salt and copper were traded.

Between 1450-1550, the Songhay kingdom grew very powerful and prosperous. It had a well-organized system of government, a developed currency and it imported fabrics from Europe. Timbuktu became one of the most important places in the world. Libraries and universities were built, and it became the meeting place for poets, scholars and artists from other parts of Africa and the Middle East.[xlvii]

Muslim chroniclers left glowing accounts of the pilgrimage of Mansa Musa and the great wealth he spread throughout the Maghreb and Levant. Coastal areas like Somali and even down to Zimbabwe developed complex societies with long range trade and urban cores, in some cases quite different than urban patterns in other parts of the world. [xlviii]

Abyssinia was a great civilization in the ancient world that is still well-known even to this day. Abyssinia is the old name for Ethiopia. There is some debate as to whether the Queen of Sheba ruled Yemen, Ethiopia, or both "the most vigorous claimant has been Ethiopia and Eritrea, where Sheba was traditionally linked with the ancient Axumite Kingdom. Owing to the connection with the Queen of Sheba, the location has thus become closely linked with national prestige, as various royal houses have claimed descent from the Queen of Sheba and Solomon." [xlix]

In some annals of history, "Ethiopia is old, even older than Egypt, but its antiquity is somewhat different. While Egypt was the world's first indisputable nation-state, unique in its complex politico-religious system augmented by magnificent material remains and a corpus of epic literature, in Ethiopia, the very cradle of humankind, the material evidence of its ancient civilization alone attests to its former glory.

The Ancient Egyptians, from the earliest times, kept records of their kings and this chronology is central to the chronological structure of the early Aegean, Levantine and Mesopotamian civilizations. It is, however, of no import to Ancient Ethiopia. If the Ethiopians did keep records, these have either been lost forever or not yet discovered. The attempts by unnamed writers to compile an Ethiopian king-list -- the Kebra Negast or Book of the Glory of Kings -- from the Queen of Sheba to the rise of the Zagwe dynasty, is believed to be a thirteenth century creation." [l]

There are several ancient structures in Africa. "The oldest standing building in Ethiopia is located in the village of Yeha: the Yeha Temple of the Moon. This is a tower built in the Sabaean style and dated through comparison with ancient structures in South Arabia to around 700 BC. Although not radiocarbon dated, the Great Tower is similar in style to structures in South Arabia around 700 BC, which makes it the oldest standing building of Africa South at the Sahara. Its "excellent state of preservation" has been attributes to its rededication - perhaps as early as the sixth century AD - for use as a Christian church." [li]

Africa's countries had many royalties. The Ethiopians had their many Emperors, the last being Haile Selassie. Somalis had their Sultans (very loose translation for Boqors, the royal families of that nation).[lii]

Nigeria had several kingdoms and civilizations. One "prominent kingdom in south western Nigeria was the Kingdom of Benin whose power lasted between the fifteenth and nineteenth century. Their dominance reached as far as the well-known city of Eko, later named Lagos by the Portuguese." [liii]

Since the beginning of humankind, the act of a few very evil people has done horrible and unspeakable things. Many civilizations or societies such the Aztec, the Mayan and the Samgoma would sacrifice people. The Romans were known to use gladiators and the Persian army of mostly slaves was forced to fight. The Egyptians enslaved a whole racial group. During the last world order, several European countries conquered, colonize and enslaved major territories around the world in the Americas, Africa, Asia, Australia, the Caribbean, New Zealand and other parts of the world. During these conquests, they murdered, raped, massacred, and pillaged the land of the indigenous people in a violent, sadistic, cruel, and barbaric manner.

Throughout the course of humankind history, we've seen empires, civilizations, societies and countries rise and fall over decades, centuries and millennia. Some of the major civilizations, empires or countries include the Ancient Egypt, Greeks and Scythians, the Arabs, the Mongol Empire, the Roman Empire, the Chinese Empire, the Empire of Alexander the Great, the Persian Empire, the Byzantine Empire, the Umayyad Caliphate and the British Empire. The Ottoman Empire was created across Mediterranean, North Africa and into South-Eastern Europe and existed during the time of European Colonization of other parts of the world.

When historians break down the major world civilizations or societies, there are over seventy, including the United States who is currently recognized as the sole remaining world power. The average length of time that a civilization or society lasts is 349.2 years. The median is 330 years. Each individual civilization contributed to the societies that exist today with new inventions, ideas, cultures, lifestyles, etc.

Empires, civilizations, societies and countries eventually vanish with starts and ends timeline, leaving only monuments and ruins. The civilizations that lasted the longest seem to be the Aksumite Empire which lasted 1100 years and the Vedic Period of India which lasted 1000 years. The shortest period is the Third Dynasty of Ur at 50 years, the Qin Dynasty at 14 years, and the Kanva Dynasty at 45 years. Byzantium as an extension of Rome lasted almost 1500 years.[liv] Based on this estimation, it seems that the average length of time for the life span of civilizations usually don't last 400 years.

The United States is presently the world's most powerful nation ever, economically and militarily speaking. The United States government is now only 243 years old. It combines the British ingenuity for trade with a more deeply held liberalism and continent-sized resources. Like the Romans, it has an attractive culture. Like the Mongols, it can wield destruction. Like the Arabs, it has spread a universal ideology across the globe. Like the Persian Empires, America combines different cultures and links together regions. Throughout the course of history, we've seen empires rise and fall over decades, centuries and even millennia. If it's true that history repeats itself, then perhaps the United States can learn from the missteps and the achievements of the world's greatest and longest lasting empires.[lv]

Typically, any political system eventually collapses, which is explained above but there are several reasons for this. Most empires, civilizations or societies regardless of the tribute system supporting them, were agriculturally reliant. Through most of human history, there have been numerous bad harvests which promote plagues and movements of large numbers of people from agricultural production. Very few political systems of a complex nature can survive these problems.

Empires, civilizations or societies invariably seem to reach a state of stagnation where their political leaders become complacent and reliant upon their previous successes and prior strategies for dealing with problems. In Arnold Toynbee's classic work 'A Study of History', he strongly makes the argument that it's this inflexibility and complacency that causes empires, civilizations or societies to fall to their neighbors eventually, or to a new dynasty that is more willing to be innovative in finding solutions to the problems that beset the polity. Often this stagnation results in a failure to adapt the economy or distribution of resources in a way that will maintain the empire. We see this is in the debasement of the Roman currency, its over-reliance on foreign military forces, and its over-expansion. The Romans failed to adapt successfully as their world changed and empire, civilizations or societies expanded.[lvi]

For many empires or societies, the greatest challenge is multi-culturalism. Several empires or societies have failed due to an inability to maintain proper respect for the various cultures within that empire. The fall of the Assyrian Empire was destroyed due to its disrespect for and brutality against subject peoples, and with the fall of the Ming dynasty to the Qing who brought the grievances of an ethnic minority into an alliance with Han Chinese elements who had lost their loyalty to the Ming.[lvii]

Sometimes empires or societies over-expand as well. The collapse of the British Empire and the conquests of Alexander the Great could be attributed to as well. Both of these empires took on more territory than they could control effectively, with Alexander managing to himself following his soldiers desire to cease and return home and the British Empire failing to address issues of multiculturalism with its efforts to maintain hegemonic control requiring a vast expenditure of wealth and resources which the British population was no longer willing to provide following WWII. The reason why the European Empires were the largest and most far flung compared to the non-European Empires, is simply because the technological advantages of the eighteenth and nineteenth centuries allowed a relatively small number of people to control a very wide area. The British Empire lasted 500 years, from the discovery of North America by John Cabot in 1497 to the handing over of Hong Kong in 1997.[lviii]

All empires or societies, at sometimes in history, will reach a point where their inept leaders take power, that's when they start to fall apart. Poor leadership leads to corrupted system which in turn, leads to anger and disloyalty of their own people, which mark the end of most empires or societies.[lix]

The Roman Empire, for example, although it lasted a long time, fell to the same pattern. The Western part of the empire suffered from a series of political turmoil of the time. Emperors came and gone, every five to ten years. This instability led to them becoming weakened from within. They could not hold the empire together when facing barbarian hordes. The Eastern Roman (Byzantine) Empire, later, met the same fate.[lx]

Another problem might be that an empire or society can lack an identity. There's no nationality, ethnicity, or religion bound to its identity. That's what may have ruined several empires or societies. Nothing lasts forever, but they all seem to follow the same path, from the Far East to the Western world.

The Transatlantic Slave Trade in the fifteenth century opened the door to a world-wide society involving colonies and empires that spread to the Americas, Asia, Australia, Africa and other territorials. Other empires, civilizations or societies were regional in nature but the European concept practical covered most of the world.

The United States is currently recognized as the sole world's remaining power with China and India lurking in the background and flexing its muscles. These large Asian markets are growing at an incredible pace but still have low income per capita. China is the globalization's present success story with the world's biggest emerging market. These countries giving attention to education, particularly in high tech fields make it conducive to expand automation and artificial intelligence. Too, China has a mostly homogeneity population and a lack of any viable leadership to the Chinese Community Party that reinforces its stability. Also, China is making a serious effort to address its issues with corruption, wealth inequality, pollution, education, safety net, medical care and others.[lxi]

The United States must deal honestly and openly with its racial and multi-culturalism issues. This has been part of the nation's DNA and the original sin since its inception. Addressing the multi-culturalism issue will be by far its greatest challenge. The United States is still considered a relatively young country compared to many nations in Europe, Asia, & Africa. It is still experiencing growing pain. The United States' ascent as a world power in such a relatively short period of time is due to a variety of reasons. The genocide of the indigenous population and taking advantage of the Transatlantic Slave Trade which offered free labor for the new country are two major reasons. Many things about America was either appropriated from an existing foreign culture or evolved into what it is today from a mingling of different racial groups and cultures that came to America for a better life or in the case with those with African descent by forced servitude.

It remains to be seen if the United States rejects multiculturalism in the long run or reassert pride in its history and national identity. Based on history, it would not be in the nation's best interest to reject multi-culturalism. It could eventually lead to its demise as a major world power, particularly when understanding the reasons for the demises and time spans of the previous world's greatest and longest lasting civilizations or societies.

PART THREE- HOW THE EXISTING WORLD RACIAL ORDER BEGUN

Between the fifteenth and nineteenth centuries, European powers attempted to wrestle control the rest of the world for all its wealth and raw materials. Through the Transatlantic Slave Trade which was part of the racial world order, they were successful in controlling large parts of the Americas, Africa, Australia, and part of Asia. Some countries, however, were able to avoid Colonization. Those ten countries are Afghanistan, Nepal, Bhutan, Ethiopia, Japan, Korea, Iran, China, Saudi, Arabia, and Thailand.[lxii]

The Atlantic Slave Trade, also known as the Transatlantic Slave Trade, was the trade of African people supplied to the Colonies of the 'new world' that occurred in and around the Atlantic Ocean. Generally, slaves were obtained through coastal trading with Africans, though some were captured by European slave traders through raids and kidnapping. Most contemporary historians estimate that approximately 9.4 to 12 million Africans arrived in the although the number of people taken from their homestead is considerably higher. The slaves were one element of a three-part economic cycle—the Triangular Trade and its Middle Passage— which ultimately involved four continents, four centuries and millions of people.

Portugal dominated and had a monopoly on the export of slaves from Africa. The country transported approximately 4.5 million African Slaves. Approximately forty percent went to the Caribbean and other forty percent went to South America with the majority (4.9 million) going to Brazil. Therefore, far more Africans ended up in South America than North America. Only a small fraction of about 450,000 was transported to the United

States. That's why black Americans only comprise thirteen percent of the United States population. Today, roughly 45 million African Americans live in the United States.

The Transatlantic Slave Trade in the fifteenth century was mainly engineered by the Portuguese in which approximately forty percent went to their Colonies on South America, mainly Brazil. The British was responsible for about twenty percent. Spain was next with approximately eighteen percent. France had about fourteen percent with Holland about four percent and Denmark with less than one percent.

Historians has estimated that 12 million African slaves entered the Transatlantic Slave Trade between the fifteenth and nineteenth centuries. About 1.5 million slaves died on the ship during the transport and 10.5 million slaves were sold into slavery, mainly in North America, South America, and the Caribbean. Another 6 million were sold to Asian slave traders and another 8 million were destined to slave markets in Africa. Four million of the slaves died in inland Africa due to diseases when trapped by opposing tribes. Most Africa slaves ended up in Brazil in which 84% worked in sugar plantations.[lxiii]

Because of the Transatlantic Slave Trade and worldwide Colonization, the United States became a European country in a non-European part of the world brought about by European migrants and African slaves. Europeans and England gave birth to America and the origins of American law. The Europeans and America are culturally similar because the United State was a child of English Colonialism. English is the shared national language and the founding fathers were of the same ethnicity. However, numerous other Europeans immigrants and Asians migrated and settled in the Americas and assimilated into society. They include the Germans, Irish, French, Italians, Polishes, Russians, Spaniards, Portuguese, Croatians, Greeks, Jews, Arabs, Chinese, Japanese, and Koreans and others.

Likewise, the continent of Australia became a European continent in a non-European part of the world. Portuguese America is today's Brazil. Brazil was settled by Portugal and the official language is Portuguese. The Spanish Colonization in Americas brought Roman Catholicism and the Spanish language to Latin America. The English Colonization brought the language to North America. France brought the French language to parts of North America (Canada and Louisiana). Protestantism came to the Americas through English Colonization. The English Colonization brought the English language in Australia, New Zealand, most of Canada and South Africa.[lxiv]

English is also one of the official languages in many African countries Nigeria, Kenya, Zimbabwe and Uganda. The Belgian Colonization has resulted in French being the official language in the Democratic Republic of Congo. Dutch and British presence in South Africa resulted in both Afrikaans and English being official languages. English is also an official language in Indian and Pakistan. Spanish is spoken in all countries south of the United States, starting with Mexico and continuing into South America, except for Brazil, where the official language is Portuguese. Portuguese is the official language in Angola and Mozambique. Those countries colonized by traditionally Roman Catholic countries (Spain and Portugal) tend to have a large proportion of Roman Catholics. The British tended to introduce Angelico Catholicism or Protestantism. The English language has spread to more countries and in some places, displaced the French and Spanish languages. There are more English-speaking countries whose primary language is not English but the second language, than there are primary language English speaking counties. [lxv]

The indigenous natives of both territories, the Indians in America and the Aborigines in Australia were mostly removed, replaced and subject to genocide. In America, most natives live on reservations and represent only 1.2 percent of the population. In Australia, Aborigines represent only 2.8 percent of the population.

The practice of slavery in Africa was common for hundreds of years prior to Transatlantic Slave Trade. The Europeans didn't have to create a new market for slaves although their demands for slaves increased astronomical after their arrival. It didn't make the practice of slavery any better, but it is important to know how history happened. Most slaves were initially captured by other Africans of a different tribe and sold to European slave traders. Europeans rarely if ever actually ventured inland to abduct Africans for the slave trade. They were for the most part already on the beaches being held by rival tribes. The vast majority of African were captured and conveyed into the hands of European slavers by their fellow Africans. The tribes and nations of the old Slave Coast became wealthy and powerful through selling their neighbors into bondage.

Forms of slavery existed in Africa before Europeans arrived. Some countries in the African continent had their own systems of slavery. People were enslaved as punishment for a crime, payment for a debt or as a prisoner of war. However, African slavery was different from what was to come later.

Most enslaved people were captured in battle.

In some kingdoms, temporary slavery was a punishment for some crimes.

In some cases, enslaved people could work to buy their freedom. Children of enslaved people did not automatically become slaves.[lxvi]

In the Transatlantic Slave Trade, slavery started soon after the discovery of the Americas (early 1500s) and ended in the 1888. The first importation of an African slave to the New World is said to have been by Juan de Cordoba, in 1502. (Many Native Americans had already been enslaved before then.)

Larger importations (shiploads of African slaves) began in 1510.

Importation of slaves was officially illegal in the United States from 1808 but continued until 1859. The Civil War started in 1861.

The United Kingdom banned the Transatlantic Slave Trade in 1807 and attempted to enforce the ban by having Royal Navy ships patrol the African coastlines. Slaves in Great Britain's American Colonies were finally freed by act of Parliament in 1833.

The various Spanish American countries (former Spanish Colonies) all abolished slavery between 1820 and 1862 (Cuba being the last to do so).

Brazil was the last Western hemisphere country to abolish slavery, in 1888. The slave trade continued until then, although it was theoretically illegal in Brazil since 1831. It also had the largest percentage of slaves from the Transatlantic Slave Trade, some thirty-five percent of the total. The Brazilian government was also under pressure from Britain, which sought to put a stop to slave trade to expand production in its own Colonies. One example is the sugar, produced both in Brazil and in the British Colonies of the West Indies; the British strove to ensure that the Brazilians would get no advantage in the world markets by using slaves.

In May 13, 1888, through the Golden Law, Princess Isabel, abolished the slavery in Brazil. The Golden Law was sanctioned by Isabel, Princess Imperial of Brazil (1846–1921), who was regent at the time, while her father, Emperor Dom Pedro II, was in Europe.

When slavery ended officially in Brazil in 1888, there was no violence over the abolition of slavery as there was in the United States. The slaveholders were given money to reimburse them for their "loss" economically.

The Transatlantic Slave Trade began in the late 1400s and finally ended in 1888.

African slaves arrived in the Americas from the following regions in the following proportions

- Senegambia (Senegal and Gambia): 4.8%

- Upper Guinea (Guinea-Bissau, Guinea and Sierra Leone): 4.1%
- Windward Coast (Liberia and Cote d' Ivoire): 1.8%
- Gold Coast (Ghana): 10.4%
- Bight of Benin (Togo, Benin and Nigeria west of the Niger Delta): 20.2%
- Bight of Biafra (Nigeria east of the Niger Delta, Cameroon, Equatorial Guinea and Gabon): 14.6%
- West Central Africa (Republic of Congo, Democratic Republic of Congo and Angola): 39.4%
- Southeastern Africa (Mozambique and Madagascar): 4.7%

Twenty-nine nation states by country that actively or passively participated in the Atlantic Slave Trade:

- Senegal: Denanke Kingdom, Kingdom of Fouta Tooro, Jolof Empire, Kingdom of Khasso and Kingdom of Saalum
- Guinea-Bissau: Kaabu Empire
- Guinea: Kingdom of Fouta Djallon
- Sierra Leone: Koya Temne
- Cote d'Ivoire: Kong Empire and Gyaaman Kingdom
- Ghana: Asante Confederacy and Mankessim Kingdom
- Benin: Kingdom of Dahomey
- Nigeria: Oyo Empire, Benin Empire and Aro Confederacy
- Cameroon: Bamun and Mandara Kingdom
- Gabon: Kingdom of Orungu
- Republic of Congo: Kingdom of Loango and Kingdom of Tio
- Angola: Kingdom of Kongo, Kingdom of Ndongo and Matamba

Over forty-five distinct ethnic groups were taken to the Americas during the trade. Of the 45, the ten most prominent according to slave documentation of the era are listed below.

1. The Gbe speakers of Togo, Ghana and Benin (Adja, Mina, Ewe, Fon)
2. The Akan of Ghana and Cote d'Ivoire
3. The Mbundu of Angola (includes Ovimbundu)
4. The BaKongo of the Democratic Republic of Congo and Angola
5. The Igbo of Nigeria
6. The Yoruba of Nigeria
7. The Mandé speakers of Upper Guinea
8. The Wolof of Senegal
9. The Chamba of Cameroon
10. The Makua of Mozambique[lxvii]

REASONS EUROPE DECIDED TO CONQUER THE WORLD

During the fifteen century, European countries decided to conquer, colonize, enslave and control the rest of the world for a variety of reasons. They will be considered below.

Europe wanted to expand its land base and empire by showing its power, strength and greed. The various countries in Europe were always battling about land and they found an enormous frontier outside their home base which offered the riches that they desired. This is like the current quest for space exploration to discover the unknown. The quest for adventure and acquisitions of new and previously occupied territories are part of humankind history. The occupied territories that they colonize did not deter the Europeans. In many instances, their methods were violent, barbaric, cruel, vicious, sadistic and destructed. Sometimes, they pillaged the land, murdered, raped and massacred many of the indigenous people.

Many Europeans came to escape persecution from religion freedom and poverty. Many came as indentured servants which was a temporary condition that afforded them the opportunity for a new beginning in a new land which they wanted to be part of. Other adventurers saw an opportunity to cultivate and work vast tracts of free land or seek what they saw as an enriched life through migration.

By expanding their European empire, they were able to obtain goods and raw materials like spices, mineral sources, furs, gold, sugar, tobacco, cocoa and other major commodities that weren't available in Europe in enough quantity. Natural resources were more plentiful in places like Africa and America.

Gunpowder was invented in China but the Europeans perfected it in their conquest of the world. By having superior weaponry and coming from a superior culture in this area, they were able to defeat the indigenous people. These technological advantages of the eighteenth and nineteenth centuries allowed a relatively small number of countries to control most of the globe. In an age before mass education and developed indigenous nationalism, there was mixed resistance from the Colonized countries. Some of the natives fought with valor and courage but the superior Europeans weaponry won the battles at the end. Also, European technology during the fifteen centuries allowed the development of ships of a quality that could transmit power to the territories to create Colonies, countries and a continent.

Many convicts from British and other Europeans countries were dispatched to America and Australia. It was a fitting destination for those who had transgressed at home.

Also, famine in Ireland during the 1840's saw huge numbers of Irish emigrants going to new Colonies. lxviii

However, it was not only European countries that took advantage of this period to colonize other parts of the world. Japan also colonized parts of China and Korea, using similar methods. The drive towards empire building has existed throughout the history of humankind. Today, countries such as the United States and China use their wealth and power to hold greater influence and access to the economic resources of other parts of the world. This is like Colonialism except without the direct rule which is no longer possible without the investment in vast expenditure.[lxix]

SLAVERY IN THE UNITED STATES, SOUTH AMERICA AND THE CARIBBEANS

Slavery came to South America and the Caribbean the same way they got to North America on slave ships. Just more went to the Caribbean and South America than came to North America. Only about 7% of the African slaves were brought to what became the US. About 40% were sent to Brazil. The rest were split among the various Caribbean and South American Colonies.

Today the Caribbean does not seem like a poor part of the world to tourists who visit its resorts and palm-fringed beaches. To them it seems far more like a luxurious paradise. Yet, one does not have to travel far beyond the hotel gates to find the same sort of poverty so visible in Africa or Asia.

Some effects of Colonization in Latin America include:

(1) Rapid spread of Christianity in the region; this replaced traditional religions

(2) Introduction of European languages (mainly Spanish, Portuguese, English, Dutch and French)

(3) Eradication of millions of natives as a result of diseases introduced by Europeans

(4) Creation of class societies were a small minority controlled the clear majority of a Colony's (or nation's) resources

(5) Division of many tribes as a result of European-created borders.

(6) Mass mining of minerals that were exported to Europe prior to independence left many new nations in the region poor.

Of the 9.4 to 12 million Africans who survived the voyage to the New World, over one-third landed in Brazil and between 60 and 70 percent ended up in Brazil or the sugar Colonies of the Caribbean. Only six percent arrived in what is now the United States. Yet by 1860, approximately two thirds of all New World slaves lived in the American South.

For a long time, it was widely assumed that southern slavery was harsher and crueler than slavery in Latin America, where the Catholic church insisted that slaves had a right to marry, to seek relief from a cruel master, and to purchase their freedom. Spanish and Portuguese colonists were thought to be less tainted by racial prejudice than North Americans and Latin American slavery was believed to be less subject to the pressures of a competitive capitalist economy.

In practice, neither the Church nor the courts offered much protection to Latin American slaves. Access to freedom was greater in Latin America, but in many cases masters freed sick, elderly, crippled, or simply unneeded slaves in order to relieve themselves of financial responsibilities.

Death rates among slaves in the Caribbean were one-third higher than in the South, and suicide appears to have been much more common. Unlike slaves in the South, West Indian slaves were expected to produce their own food in their "free time," and care for the elderly and the infirm.

The largest difference between slavery in the South and in Latin America was demographic. The slave population in Brazil and the West Indies had a lower proportion of female slaves, a much lower birthrate, and a higher proportion of recent arrivals from Africa. In striking contrast, southern slaves had an equal sex ratio, a high birthrate, and a predominantly American-born population.

Slavery in the United States was especially distinctive in the ability of the slave population to increase its numbers by natural reproduction. In the Caribbean, Dutch Guiana, and Brazil, the slave death rate was so high and the birthrate so low that slaves could not sustain their population without imports from Africa. The average number of children born to an early nineteenth-century southern slave woman was 9.2—twice as many as in the West Indies.

In the West Indies, slaves constituted 80 to 90 percent of the population, while in the South only about a third of the population was enslaved. Plantation size also differed widely. In the Caribbean, slaves were held on much larger units, with many plantations holding 150 slaves or more. In the American South, in contrast, only one slaveholder held as many as a thousand slaves, and just 125 had over 250 slaves. Half of all slaves in the United States worked on units of twenty or fewer slaves; three-quarters had fewer than fifty.

These demographic differences had important social implications. In the American South, slaveholders lived on their plantations and slaves dealt with their owners regularly. Most planters placed plantation management, supply purchasing, and supervision in the hands of black drivers and foremen, and at least two-thirds of all slaves worked under the supervision of black drivers. Absentee ownership was far more common in the West Indies, where planters relied heavily on paid managers and on a distinct class of free blacks and mulattos to serve as intermediaries with the slave population.

Another important difference between Latin America and the United States involved conceptions of race. In Spanish and Portuguese America, an intricate system of racial classification emerged. Compared with the British and French, the Spanish and Portuguese were much more tolerant of racial mixing—an attitude encouraged by a shortage of European women—and recognized a wide range of racial gradations, including black, mestizo, quadroon, and octoroon. The American South, in contrast, adopted a two-category system of race in which any person with a black mother was automatically considered to be black.[lxx]

"In Latin America, indigenous people were subject to genocide but not to the comparable proportions found in North America. When the Spanish conquistadores came to the Western Hemisphere, they brought no women with them. Intermarriage became common, and, therefore, Indians were not considered to be uncivilized subhuman. On the other hand, the British, French, and Dutch who settled in North America brought their families with them. Their primary contact with the American Indians involved fighting against those who resisted the European settlers' encroachment on their land.

A similar contract existed with respect to slavery. In Latin America, slaves were considered to be unfortunate human beings who temporarily found themselves in a difficult situation. They were never considered subhuman property to be treated as objects. Families were not divided. Many slaves were able to buy their freedoms with work or money.

Conversely, in the United States there existed one of the most inhumane forms of slavery in history. Slaves were considered property no different than livestock, to be bought and sold without regard for family ties. The women were frequently sexually assaulted, and the men thoroughly emasculated. In order to train them for slavery, every effort was made to systematically destroy the language, awareness of history, religion, culture, customs, and family structure of these African people. It was also illegal to teach them to read.

These differences account for the much higher degree of racism, prejudice, and discrimination prevalent in the United States. Fortunately, some progress has been made during the past decades, but a lot of work remains in race relations. [lxxi]

SLAVERY IN CANADA

The history of slave trading in Canada is a little-known fact by most people. Despite the small percentage of slaves in Canada compared to other countries in the Americas; but long before the underground railroad got started, it was a safe place to buy, sell and own slaves.

Like America, Canada was built in part by slave labor, centered mainly in New France, which is now known as the province of Quebec. Thousands of African and Aboriginal people were sold into bondage, either bought from traders overseas, traded between the French and the British, or even sold by Aboriginal people themselves, who had little other use for those captured in wars between various tribes.

Between 1671 and 1833, around 4,000 slaves were held captive in Canada, two-thirds of whom were First Nations people and the rest mainly African. Most of those held in captivity were very young, between the ages of 14 and 18 years old. All were forced to serve the political and social elite of the times, and although their treatment was much better than that endured by American slaves, they still enjoyed little freedom and endured the pain of being separated from their families and culture.

The main reason the slave trade in Canada did not balloon to the proportions seen in the United States was the principle differences in industry between the two nations at the time. Canada's main source of income was the fur trade, an industry served primarily by hunters, and Canada's farming industry was not focused on exportation, unlike the massive cotton industry in the US. Slaves were also very expensive during this period—even an unskilled slave cost as much as four times an average person's annual income. That said, the abhorrent practice did exist in Canada and affected thousands, leaving an often-unmentioned scar on the nation's psyche.[lxxii]

Unlike other countries, Canada did not end its slavery. In 1777, slaves began fleeing Canada for Vermont, which had just abolished slavery. It took Great Britain to finally outlaw the practice across their entire empire in 1834.[lxxiii]

THE COLONIZATION OF AFRICA

The European powers decided to colonize the continent of Africa for economic, political, and religious motives during the 1800s and propelled several European countries to colonize Africa. The European countries such as Great Britain, France, Germany, Belgium, Spain, Portuguese, Italy and other powers were suffering from economic depression. The continent of Africa appeared to be a way out of their depression. Africa had an abundant of natural resources and raw goods which allowed the European country to expand their economy. The industrial revolution was also making progress, making those goods of the utmost importance. These materials could possibly spark a financial boom in Europe. During that time, a main goal of countries was to become self-sufficient. They weren't interested in trading with any other European countries. Basically, having Colonies allowed countries to obtain wealth and seem powerful.

Another reason for the Colonization of Africa was because of rivalries between countries. Britain and France had conflict with each other for centuries due to the infamous one hundred years war. Great Britain and France and other European powers (Germany, Italy and Spain) benefited and wanted to compete against each other in Africa and dividing the different countries as Colonies. Nationalism was quite popular in many Western European countries, everyone wanted their country to be the strongest. [lxxiv]

The Europeans had a dramatic effect on the cultural traditions of Africans through assimilation. Africans were acculturated in almost every area of their culture. Colonial rulers had every expectation that the countries they ruled should model the cultural traditions of Europeans. They viewed Africans as culturally inferior. As a result, cultural characteristics like language and religion changed for Africa.

Many Africans learned the European languages, so they would have the opportunity for economic mobility. Christian missionaries flooded the continent to convert Africans to Christianity. Christianity has been the fastest growing religion in Africa since the 19th Century while the amount of people practicing traditional religions has declined significantly.

Africans did not traditionally have formal educations systems. Europeans introduced formal systems to train Africans to partake in the Colonial process. The education of Africans was not done for their benefit, but to indoctrinate a segment of the population that could be mobilized to assist in the political, social, and economic exploitation of Africa.

In most Colonies in Africa, the Europeans utilized existing government systems and leadership. The natives that worked in the government but did not have any real autonomy or sovereignty. The village leaders would govern for the European power. This collaboration had economic and political benefits for Africans in these positions. This indirect system of rule caused a lot of resentment between African groups, which ultimately led to civil wars.

While Africans were often denied the right to vote, they had access to medicines and education that weren't available prior to colonization. Better farming practices meant that famines dissipated in those countries with European Colonials. Colonization also saw the rise of modern cities in sub-Saharan Africa including railways, airports and major roads all linking people together. Europeans would find it easier to do this in the 1800's because of new improvements in technology. The Maxim gun, an early edition of the machine gun, was far superior to the native tribes' muskets or spears. Many native religions were severely impacted or eliminated such as the Ibo and the Swahili religions. There were also new advances in medicine, allowing (to an extent) Europeans to better survive malaria and yellow fever.[lxxv]

THE COLONIZATION OF ASIA

When you compare European Colonial incursions into the Americas, Australia, New Zealand and Africa, the people in Asia were already vastly advanced. The Europeans had a more difficult time trying to colonize these territories. In fact, the military superiority of some in Asia caused great delays to European exploitation. The population and the culture were already in place. The Europeans monopolized and utilize the trading and shipping bases in the various countries.

The major colonizers of Southeast Asia were Europeans, Japanese and the United States. All in all, there were seven Colonial powers in Southeast Asia: Portugal, Spain, the Netherlands, Great Britain, France, the United States, and Japan. From the 1500s to the mid-1940s, Colonialism was imposed over Southeast Asia.

For hundreds of years, Southeast Asian kingdoms had been engaged in international commercial relations with traders from East Asia (China), South Asia (India), and West Asia (the "Middle East"). Asian sojourners also brought religion, customs, traditions, and court practices to the region. Hence, their relationship was economic and cultural at the same time. Moreover, local Southeast Asian rulers used and indigenized practices of kingship institutions from South Asia and West Asia.

European travelers did not only have economic relations with Southeast Asians but also imposed their political—and in some cases, cultural—domination over Southeast Asian peoples and territories. Hence, European Colonialism covered a large chunk of Southeast Asian history.

Aside from European Colonials, Japanese and United States Colonials controlled much of Southeast Asia. Japanese aggression took place during the "Pacific War" of World War II. The Japanese occupied much of Asia, including Southeast Asia. The United States colonized the Philippines in the aftermath of the Spanish-American War of 1898.[lxxvi] Portugal, the Netherlands, France, and Great Britain colonized India but by 1856, it was mostly controlled by Great Britain, except for Goa which was controlled by Portugal. Portugal and the Netherlands colonized Sri Lanka (known as Ceylon back then), but it went to Great Britain in 1815. France colonized North Vietnam, Cambodia, and Laos. Great Britain colonized Hong Kong and Burma. Southeast Asia response to Colonialism was both collaboration and nationalism in all its forms.[lxxvii]

THE CONQUEST AND COLONIZATION OF AUSTRALIA AND NEW ZEALAND

The British explorers first set foot on the continent of Australia in 1788. They arrived on a small fleet of boats with over a thousand people of which many were convicts. The British settled this Great Southland in 1788, when Captain Arthur Phillip landed upon the shores of Botany Bay where they were planning to set up a settlement. Admiral James Cook provided a report about the isolated continent in 1780 and encouraged the expedition. Anyway, penal Colonies away from Britain were established for convicts where they would serve their sentence. Gradually widespread migration from Europe was endorsed by the government.

This was also the time that the Aboriginal war started, between the natives of Australia and the British who encroach on the Aboriginal people's living environment. The early settlers from Great Britain settled in what is known as Sidney, Australia.

By the late 1700's, the European powers were engaging in competition with each other to extend their empires across the world. The British was competing against the French to colonize and conquer Australia. The British first established Australia as a penal colony for its wayward citizens. They wanted to solve their problems with their overcrowded prisons due to the Industrial Revolution. More than 170,000 criminals, from Britain, arrived in Australia in 1868. Because the prisoners were English speaking they turned Australia into an English-speaking nation. This also led to the language known as Strine, which describes the accent Australian's have when speaking English. But like all the other European colonies, they were interested in the continent's riches of raw materials which Australia had to offer. They also wanted to gain more power and territory, extend their naval power and the location of Australia provided proximity to trade with China from the East. The continent had a strategic position and a great geographical location. At the time, the English were at war with the Netherlands, who had control over Indonesia and several small fragment islands. The Dutch East India Company were centered here, and Britain could use Australia as a good area to block trading vessels from docking. Often the Dutch sailed by the East coast, an example is the Batavia in 1629. Keep in mind it is also bordered by water from all sides - very hard to attack effectively, as the land itself is so huge.

During 1804 the British flag was raised in Tasmania. In addition to this all British settlers were ordering to shoot and kill all Aboriginals on sight. No matter of age, gender or health. This resulted in the last full-blooded Tasmanian dying in 1876. This shows the British attempt to take over Tasmania and claim it as their own, even though many other people had lived there for many years before. It shows the Eurocentrism of the British. It also shows the point where tensions between the British and Aboriginal people began to boil over. Before colonization, there were about 300,000 Aborigines living in Australia. They spoke about 500 languages but didn't have a written language. They told their culture through songs and artwork. In addition to the natural resources been depleted by the British invasion, the culture of the Aboriginals was destroyed. The indigenous people were dispossessed, leading to a conflict within our society that is still unresolved.

Aboriginals suffered significantly initially. There is a strong debate among historians as to whether there was a deliberate genocide policy which cannot be proven. In 1837 the British parliamentary committee accused Aussies of purposely killing natives. This cannot be confirmed and with lack of evidence, probably will never be. Aborigines lost a lot of their original culture because of much devastation. It has affected generations of Aboriginals. Christianity was brought to the continent replacing their native religions such as Mayan, Aztecs, etc.

In 1823, conflict between the British and the Aboriginals became so heated that the British proclaimed martial law. This forced the citizens of Australia to follow the laws of the British Military. In addition, ship owners and whalers in Australia called for British intervention on explorers selling guns to the Maori people. The reason behind this was the whalers wanted to minimize conflict with Maori as tensions between the groups were high. This also led to Australia's first Parliament and criminal and civil courts. The first Parliament and criminal and civil courts moved Australia toward a more independent, self-reliant country.

In 1868: Criminal Australia - This shows Britain's view of Australia, being, a land mass capable of holding criminals and nothing more. It also signifies Australia as an English-speaking country, eliminating all other Aboriginal languages, turning it into a more European country. It also forced the Australian people previously living there to have to deal with the social, political and economic effects of the British influence. It was not until 1967 that Harold Holt held the referendum to change the constitution. This altered phrases from section 51 and 127, which stated Aborigines required special laws to govern them. Basically, the revision of the document assured them full citizenship rights. Currently, the opportunities, freedom and privileges for Aboriginals are within their own capable hands. They have been the given the ability to create their own destiny and live in a prosperous, rich society which is the total opposite before Colonization.

A totally unique culture emerged, surfacing from a profound sense of nationalism. Australia was declared a separate entity from the Motherland in 1901, when they became a federation. Their attitudes, beliefs, customs and values had all changed over the lengthy 120 years period.

On January 1st, 1901 Australia became a self-governing member of the British Empire. This joined the six previous Colonies of South Australia, Tasmania, Victoria, Western Australia, New South Wales and Queensland into one country. January 1st is now known as Australia day. This marks the end of British Imperialism in Australia. Now that Australia is a self-governing country they can do what is best for them, politically, economically and socially, as opposed to what is best for the British monarchy.[lxxviii]

In 1840, Britain formally annexed the islands and New Zealand's first permanent European settlement was established on 22 January 1840. New Zealand was initially part of the Australian Colony of New South Wales. It became a separate colony in 1841 and became self-governing in 1852.

There are similarities and differences between Australia and New Zealand. One similarity is that both countries were Colonies of Great Britain at one time. Both countries are island nations in the South Pacific. There is also a free movement of people between the two countries. There are many Australians that live in New Zealand and many New Zealanders who live in Australia. While Britain colonized both countries, the essential difference is that in Australia the earliest settlers were convicts of penial colonies whereas New Zealand was populated by free settlers, mainly whalers, sealers, and missionaries. In New Zealand, some of the earliest settlers were missionaries. They wanted to convert the indigenous people, called Maori. They were humanitarian; so, they created a treaty, the Treaty of Waitangi where the British crown held sovereignty but allowed the Maori to own their own land and let them enjoy rights as if they were British citizens.

New Zealand became a British Colony in 1840 with the signing of the Treaty of Waitangi. Afterward, many more free settlers from Britain arrived in New Zealand. Whereas Britain recognized the rights of the Maori people and saw the need to establish a treaty with them before they colonized the country, they did not recognize the rights of the Australian Aborigines and settled the country regardless.

Both countries have similarities and differences even though the British ruled both of them at the same time, and these countries are not that far from each other. There are differences between these two countries. Australia was created as a place for convicts to live. The earliest settlers in New Zealand were the Maori who came from eastern Polynesia. New Zealand receives more rainfall than Australia, which makes farming easier to do. Australia has a larger population than New Zealand. Both countries have had Chinese people migrate there. In Australia, the Chinese have been more likely to give up their ethnic identity than in New Zealand.[lxxix]

MODERN SLAVERY

Today, all governments in the world have banned slavery but it remains a huge problem. From a global perspective, slavery has never been fully abolished although it's illegal in most countries. There are more slaves today than ever before in the world. By some estimates, up to 40 to 50 million people live-in modern-day bondage.

Modern slavery in numbers:

- 10 million children are in slavery across the world
- 30.4 million people are in slavery in the Asia-Pacific region, mostly in bonded labor
- 9.1 million people are in slavery in Africa
- 2.1 million people are in slavery in The Americas
- 1.5 million people are in slavery in developed economies
- 16 million slavery victims are exploited in economic activities
- 4.8 million people are in forced into sexual exploitation
- 99% of people trafficked for sexual exploitation are women and girls
- 4.1 million people in slavery are exploited by governments
- US$ 150 billion – illegal profits forced labor in the private economy generates per year
- *All estimates by ILO[lxxx]

"The modern-day estimate for the number of men, women and children forced into labor worldwide exceeds 40m. Today's global slave trade is so lucrative that it nets traffickers more than US$150 billion each year. Slavery affects children as well as adults

Debt bondage often ensnares both children and adults. In Haiti, for example, many children are sent to work by their families as domestic servants under what's known as the Restavek system –

the term comes from the French language rester avec, "to stay with". These children, numbering as many as 300,000, are often denied an education, forced to work up to 14 hours a day and are sometimes victims of sexual abuse.

Slavery is not always race based. Then, as now, race is not always the main reason for enslaving someone. In the past, those who were living in poverty, who did not have the protection of kinship networks, those displaced by famine, drought or war were often caught up in slavery.

In the United Kingdom, nail salons, restaurants, music festivals and farms have all be found to have people working in slavery. Victims of human trafficking come from all parts of the world and all walks of life. There isn't just one type of modern-day slavery, it takes many forms.

The demand for certain types of goods has propelled slavery's numbers. In the past, the desire for sugar drove the growth in slavery. Now, the global consumption of electronic goods has exacerbated slavery in the Coltan mines of the Democratic Republic of Congo. Many slaves or trafficked victims are often exploited in mining for gold, coltan, molybdenum, niobium, tin – which can be used in electronic goods sold around the world.

According to Save the Children, 5,000 to 6,000 young children work in the Coltan mining industry, surrounded by armed guards to prevent their escape. Much of the profit from this trade goes to fund ongoing militia warfare in Central Africa. Slavery is a daily reality for 10m children around the world.

Chattel slavery (where one person is the property of another) is illegal but still exists especially in the West African country of Mauritania – where abolitionists' efforts to stamp out the practice have been in vain.

The organization Fight Slavery Now says that today at least 90,000 Mauritanians are the property of others, while up to

600,000 men, women and children are in a bonded labor situation – up to 20% of the population.

India has the greatest number of slaves globally. India has the highest number of slaves in the world, with estimates ranging from 14m to 18m people. In India many people work as slave labor in the brick kiln industry – this includes women and children.

Now, as in the past, not all slaves are forced into slavery. Historically, some experienced such severe poverty that they had no choice but to sell themselves to be bound to another person. And similar cases still happen around the world today.

It involves global movement. Long distance movement is common in slavery of the past and the present. For West Africans in the pre-modern era, the journey across the Atlantic must have been unimaginable.

Today, laborer's move around the world freely looking for work, but some end up caught in slavery-like situations. They are promised a good job with decent conditions and wages, but instead are trapped in a cycle of debt and despair, where they are bound to their employer with no chance of escape.

In recent years, at least 30,000 children have been abducted and forced to labor in the Lord's Resistance Army led by Joseph Kony, in Northern Uganda.

Slavery still exists in many forms today, and the impacts it has on millions of people are no less devastating than they were in the past." [lxxxi]

About 50 percent toil in forced labor slavery in industries where manual labor is needed—such as farming, ranching, logging, mining, fishing, and brick making—and in-service industries working as dish washers, janitors, gardeners, and maids. About 12.5 percent are trapped in forced prostitution sex slavery. About 37.5 percent are trapped in forced marriages and bout 25 percent of today's slaves are children.[lxxxii]

TRANSATLANTIC SLAVE TRADE – TIMELINE FOR SLAVE BAN

1440- 1500
West Africa - Portugal
1502- 1580
Central Africa- South America
1580- 1850
West Africa - Caribbean & North America
Central Africa- South America & central, Caribbean & North America
West Africa- Europe
Denmark stopped in 1803
Britain banned the slave trade in 1807
United States outlawed importation of slaves in 1808
The last recorded slave ship to land on American soil was the Clotilde, which in 1859 illegally smuggled several Africans into the town of Mobile, Alabama. The Africans on board were sold as slaves, however slavery was abolished 5 years later following the end of the civil war. The last survivor of the voyage was Cudjoe Lewis who died in 1935.

ABOLISHMENT OF SLAVE TRADE IMPORTATION

Denmark 1803
Britain & rest of Europe 1807 (including Spain, Denmark, Netherlands & France)
USA 1808
Brazil 1831

ABOLISHMENT OF TRANSATLANTIC SLAVE TRADE ENDING TIMELINE

Portugal: 1761
Central Great Lakes Region of the United States: 1787
Haiti: 1791
Upper Canada: 1793
Lower Canada: In 1803
Argentina: 1813
Ecuador, Colombia, Panama, and Venezuela: 1821
Guatemala, El Salvador, Honduras, Nicaragua and Costa Rica: 1824
Mexico: 1829
British Empire: 1833
Denmark: 1848,
France: 1848
Peru: 1851
Colombia: 1853
Venezuela: 1854
Netherlands: 1863
United States :1865
Puerto Rico: 1873
Cuba: 1886
Jamaica: 1832
Brazil: 1888
Sierra Leone: 1928
Ghana: 1930
Thailand: 1915
Iran: 1928[lxxxiii]

THE TIMELINE FOR ABOLISHING SLAVERY IN THE EUROPEAN COUNTRIES

Slavery in the United States was different from what it was in Europe. The Europeans had slaves for centuries and millennia coming from different groups of peoples such as Jews and Serfs.

Later European countries captured slaves from Africa and shipped them to their North American colonies, so there may have been times when there was no slavery within the European countries.

France abolished slavery in 1795 but it was re-established sometime afterwards after a revolt in 1802. It was then made illegal again in 1848.

Britain made it illegal in the British Empire in 1807 even though it was already illegal in England and Wales in 1772 (in practice) and Scotland in 1776

Hungary declared any slave free as soon as they entered the Hungarian boarders around the year 1000.

Sweden abolished slavery in 1847 with the last slaves being made free in 1848.

Spain made it illegal in 1837 but only for the country itself, not for any of its colonies.

Portugal: 1761

Denmark and its colonies: 1848.

Russia: 1861 (although the USSR which came afterwards had forced labor camps)

The Netherlands and its colonies: 1863.

Germany forced labor in concentration camps until they were defeated in 1945 and these camps were liberated.

Abolition of slavery started in the United Kingdom in 1789 and continued until through 1790 until 1792.

The dates varied, but mostly ranged from the late 1700s to about the 1840s, except for Turkey. They were the only country to still legally allow slavery longer than the US.

1117: Iceland abolishes slavery
1772: England
1847: Sweden (and Finland, which was part of Sweden at the time)
1588: Lithuania
1723: Russia
1761 and 1777: Portugal
1778: Scotland
1783: Ukraine-Romania region
1807: British Empire
1807: Prussia (Germany)
1811: Spain
1818: Holland
1818: France
1822: Greece
1848: Denmark
1855: Moldovia (Part of Romania)
1856: Wallachia (Part of Romania)[lxxxiv]

PART FOUR - IDENTIFYING PAST AND PRESENT GLOBAL RACIAL INEQUALITY

Below is a synopsis of an incomplete list of major racial inequalities in the United States and around the world. The issues occurred during the existing world racial order when several European countries decided during the fifteenth centuries to colonize, enslave and conquer most of the world. These inequalities which were formed by historical racial constructs, force us to come to terms with the global implications of racial oppression. It is important to consider global racism and inequality in context, to understand the historical and cultural influences that have brought us to this point in world history.

History is full of inequalities like some of the ones mentioned below. To cover all the inequalities in history would be realistically impossible. This is why most historians tend to focus on a period of history. You simply cannot cover all of them in detail. Many of the present global racial inequalities still enforce the foundation of the foundation of the Transatlantic Slave Trade and world-wide Colonization the Holocaust and Apartheid. These racial issues and inequalities that are played out today in society and the media are a continuous manifestation of the original sins of the Europeans-Americans.

Many of these ensuing race-based inequalities manifested themselves in public policies and laws world-wide that were implemented along racial lines. For example, "the Japanese Internment camps during World War II existed in the United States and Canada where Japanese-Americans were herded into relocation centers but not German-Americans. The Louisiana territory was purchased from the French, and Alaska from the Russians, but the United States took California, Arizona, New

Mexico and Texas from Mexicans who are subordinate group members."[lxxxv]

Presently, in the United States, immigration issues, particular with Mexico and Latin American countries have developed into a hotly contested political debate, including the proposal to build a boundary wall at the Southern U.S. border to keep illegal immigrants out of the country. However, illegal immigrants and terrorist threats from Canada at the Northern border should also be a concern. Some Canadians let the visas expired and remain in the United States as illegal immigrants far outpace immigration issues at the Southern border. However, this issue is rarely discussed in a public discourse because most Canadians are members of the dominant culture.

It should be noted that many of the aforementioned listed racial inequalities are not isolated stand-alone issues in countries around the world. The dominant culture carefully crafted an organized calculated network of intertwined racial issues that existed in many countries during the same time frames that were designed to keep subordinate groups under their control. Many of the issues manifested themselves in public policies and laws world-wide. For example, the Japanese Internment camps during World War II existed in the United States and Canada; the genocide of the indigenous people occurred in the Americas, Africa, Asia, Australia and New Zealand; the human zoos existed in many countries in Europe and the United States; affirmative action and eugenics issues are debated in many countries throughout the world; the Chinese inclusion (Head Tax) acts were passed in several countries; Indian Boarding schools were implemented in the United States and Canada; and segregated housing and public schools patterns are prevalent in all global societies. A few will be considered below.

1. **The Genocide of Native Americans** – a deliberate, calculated and insidious attempt at destroying the natives. It is considered to be one of the most horrific genocides known to man. Before the European invasion, it has been estimated that there were between nine and eighteen million indigenous people by some accounts in North America. By the end of the Indian Wars in the 1890's, there were about 250,000 in what is now called the United States.

There were about 123,000 in what is now Canada. Canada's first prime minister, John A. MacDonald, is a historical figure akin to the founding fathers of the United States. He has had many monuments erected in his honor and even adorns the Canadian $10 bill. However, many don't know that he instigated a campaign of forced starvation against the Aboriginal peoples of Canada during his term as the head of the newly founded nation. Under his tenure, he oversaw a government policy to withhold food from Aboriginal peoples until they moved to dictated reservations. Even after they complied, their food supply was stored in ration houses and still denied to them, left to rot as the people starved.[lxxxvi] The way it happened was unconscionable.

2. **Japanese American internment** – following the Japanese attack on Pearl Harbor, Hawaii, on 7 December 1941during World War II, Japanese internment camps (also called War Relocation Camps) were set up in parts of Canada and the United States.

On February 19, 1942, soon after the beginning of World War II, Franklin D. Roosevelt signed Executive Order 9066. The evacuation order commenced the round-up of 120,000 Americans of Japanese heritage to one of 10 internment camps—officially called "relocation centers"—in California, Idaho, Utah, Arizona, Wyoming, Colorado, and Arkansas. Thousands of Japanese Americans were relocated to these internment camps which were disbanded in 1945.[lxxxvii]

Japanese Americans living in the western states were arrested and removed to a series of "relocation centers" in isolated interior locations. Two-thirds of this group were United States citizens, and most of the rest had been denied the right of citizenship because they were not born in the country. The sole criterion for removal was their Japanese ancestry.

Just over 90 per cent of Japanese Canadians — some 21,000 people — were uprooted during the war. The majority were Canadian citizens by birth. In 1946, nearly 4,000 former internees sailed to a bombed-out Japan. About 2,000 were aging first-generation immigrants — 1,300 were children under 16 years of age. The last controls on Japanese Canadians were not lifted until 1948, when they were granted the right to vote. Finally, Canadian society began to open to the Japanese. [lxxxviii]

3. **Philippine-American War** - was an armed military conflict between the United States of America and the First Philippine Republic, fought between 1899 to at least 1902, which arose from a Filipino political struggle against U.S. occupation of the Philippines.

4. **Jim Crow laws** – state and local laws enacted primarily but not exclusively in the southern and border states between 1876 and 1965. They mandated segregation in all public facilities with a 'separate but equal' status for African Americans and members of the dominant group. In addition to racism, a persuasive argument has been made that these laws were made to create a divide among working class whites and blacks out of fear by the elitism that they would join together for a common cause. The Jim Crow laws in the United States are discussed further in part five.

5. **Cherokee Trail of Tears** – in 1930, President Andrew Jackson signed into law, the Indian Removal Act, which authorized and allowed of five Indian tribes (Cherokee, Choctaw, Muscogee, (Creek), Chickasaw and Seminole) to Indian Territory to modern day Oklahoma from southeast United States to open up land for the European settlers. There were approximately 11 of these trails, taken by different tribes based upon location and thousands of

Indians died. They ranged in distances from 200 to 900 miles and went through 14 states.

6. **Crime** - The misrepresentation of crime statistics has always been a main propaganda point of the dominant culture. Unsubstantiated views about the potential violence from black people was the number one excuse or reason to justify slavery, Jim Crow laws and mass incarceration. But never was the Klux Klan (KKK) violence or the lynching of black people by white people ascribed to an inherent white or group trait.

Africa Americans are always represented higher in crime statistics as broadly reported by the media. That may be true depending upon what source of crime data you review and interpret. However, Africa Americans' crime is almost always a result of socio-economic inequality and poverty. America has five percent of the world's population yet twenty-five percent of those incarcerated. Politicians in both major parties are aware of the disparate treatment involving Africa Americans in its criminal justice system and actively working to reform it at all levels of government.

By taking crime statistics at face value, blaming higher rates of black crime on an innate black criminality, when in fact those disproportionate crime rates could be explained by poverty and related structural disadvantages. On average, African Americans and Latinos were — and remain — far poorer and more likely to live in disadvantaged neighborhoods than whites. Police view their responsibilities to different neighborhoods. These produce exceedingly elevated arrest, conviction and incarceration rates for black and Latino men. Concentrated poverty has a criminogenic effect: lack of access to jobs, increased idle time and poorer educational opportunities all increase one's chances of engaging in criminal behavior, and the effect is the same for black and white people. One study, released three years before The Color of Crime, found that when sociologists controlled for structural disadvantages, there were no significant differences between crime rates in black and white communities.[lxxxix]

All races commit crimes. Out of 90% of all murders in America black people make up 50% percent which is to say that black people make up 45% of the 90%. Black murders are black males killing black males. 84% of whites murdered in the United States are murdered by other whites. 36% of those murders are white women being murdered by white males. The point here is that just like there is black on black crime the same can be said about white on white crime in America. The media is always talking about black on black crimes, but it never mentions white on white crimes. Eighty-five percent of white people that killed in America each year are murdered by other white people. "Black on black crime" is a term that has been specifically for African Americans to create feelings of self-hatred and disunity within the racial group. That's a double standard because whites' control most of the media locally, nationally and international.

7. **The Middle Passage** - It was the movement of African slaves across the Atlantic Ocean during the fifteenth to nineteenth centuries. They were moved from Africa to the Americas and Caribbean to work on plantations. The Middle Passage was the brutal and horrific transportation of Africans across the Atlantic to the plantations of the Caribbean and Americas. Africans were captured and imprisoned in forts, or barracoons on the west African coastline before enduring the inhumane conditions of the Middle Passage.

8. **The History of European American racism** – global racism is worldwide, covers all ages and stems from previous racism in Africa, the Mediterranean, Europeans, Asians and the Americas. So, its roots are deeply entrenched around the world. The history of the European-American racism beginning with the Transatlantic Slave Trade is discussed in part three.

9. **Black Codes** - the Black Codes were laws passed on the state and local level in the United States to limit the basic human rights and civil liberties of blacks. The term Black Codes is used most often to refer to legislation passed by Southern states at the end of the Civil War to control the labor, migration and other activities of newly-freed slaves. The intent of the legislation was to reaffirm the inferior position that slaves and free African Americans had held in the antebellum South and to regulate black labor. The Black Codes in the United States are discussed further in part five.

10. **Slave Patrols** - the slave patrols were an organized group of elected sheriffs and local militias who monitored and enforce discipline whose primary function was to police slaves, especially runaways and defiant slaves. They also formed river patrols to prevent escape by boat. Slave patrols were first established in South Carolina in 1704, and the idea spread throughout the Colonies. But policing in British North America predates the slave patrols by about 75 years in the Colonial period. [xc]

11. **Ku Klux Klan** - a secret terrorist organization that originated in the Southern states during the period of Reconstruction following the American Civil War (1861-1865) and was reactivated on a wider geographic basis in the 20th century. The original Klan was organized in Pulaski, Tennessee, during the winter of 1865 to 1866, by six former Confederate army officers who gave their society a name adapted from the Greek word kilos ("circle"). Although the Ku Klux Klan began as a prankish social organization, its activities soon were directed against the Republican Reconstruction governments and their leaders, both black and white, which came into power in the South in 1867. The Ku Klux Klan is a white supremacist group created in the mid 1800's that sole purpose was to spread the idea that white, Christian men were superior to any other kind of people. They wore white clothing, hoods, and masks to hide their identity and usually terrorized blacks, Jews, and subordinate group members.

They commonly practiced burning crosses in their victim's lawn and lynching targets. They began to up-rise in large numbers in the South due to blacks being freed from slavery. They still exist today but are considered a terrorist group in the United States, have little funding, and a decreasing membership demand each year. [xci]

12. **The War on Drugs** - was started in its broadest sense, in 1880, when the U.S. and China completed an agreement (see Opium wars) that prohibited the shipment of opium between the two countries. Over the past 149 years, billions of dollars have been spent on this war and it has not been won. The war on drugs a term given to the actions by the United States government to combat the production and distribution of illegal drugs. The term was popularized following a letter to congress from President Nixon, in which he declared illegal drugs to be "public enemy number one". This war disproportionately targets African Americans and other subordinate group members and the poor across all racial demographics.[xcii]

13. **Treaty of Guadalupe Hidalgo** - is the peace treaty, largely dictated by the United States to the interim government of a militarily occupied Mexico City, that ended the Mexican-American War (1846 – 48) on February 2, 1848. With the defeat of its army and the fall of the capital, Mexico surrendered to the United States and entered into negotiations to end the war. The land that the Treaty of Guadalupe Hidalgo brought into the United States became, between 1850 and 1912, all or part of ten States: California (1850), Nevada (1864), Utah (1896), and Arizona (1912), as well as the whole of, depending upon interpretation, the entire State of Texas (1845) that then included part of Kansas (1861), Colorado (1876), Wyoming (1890), Oklahoma (1902), and New Mexico (1912).[xciii]

14. **How White Racism Grew out of Slavery and Genocide** - throughout the history of humankind, all human beings have at

least some degree of in-group/out-group bias, but if/when it's greater in a particular group it's probably a choice of the racial group and part of their cultural phenomenon.

Race, which leads to racism led to slavery and genocide. Therefore, slavery was a symptom of racism. However, continued examples of inequalities after slavery and the genocide of the indigenous people by the dominant cultures against the subordinate groups based on genetic makeup and lineage provide another point toward the idea that slavery was a predecessor of European-American racism.

15. **Jewish Holocaust** - the subjugation and persecution of the Jews has been a major part of European history for at least the past thousand years as Hitler needed a common enemy to unite Germany behind according to a popular theory. The Holocaust is the name applied to the state-led systematic persecution and genocide of the Jews and other minority groups of Europe and North Africa during World War II by Nazi Germany and its collaborators. The commonly used figure for the number of Jewish victims is six million, though estimates by historians using, among other sources, records from the Nazi regime itself, range from five million to eleven million. The holocaust is discussed further in part five.

16. **White Anti-racism** - it's a phase that means being against discrimination towards non-whites actually negatively effects white people, therefore the term anti-racism means anti-white. It means anyone who is against racism and support multiculturalism and miscegenation (race-mixing)

17. **The Southern strategy** - refers to the Republican Party's strategy of gaining political support and power by winning elections in the Southern United States by appealing to racism against African Americans. The Southern states were targeted for votes by playing the dominant culture fears and anger over the end of segregation.

18. **The Rape of Enslaved Women** - this was done for various reasons but sometimes slave owners did it in a display of power and dominion. To show who was in charge. They also did it to emasculate the enslaved African men, remove them from the forefront of the family, to disrupt the unity found in the African families by raping their wives in front of them. They also did it to increase the slave population, including their own children.

19. **Madison Grant** - was an American scientific racist and conservationist. In 1916 he wrote the book that Hitler called his Bible: "The Passing of the Great Race", a best-seller in America. He helped to shape American laws on immigration, marriage and even deer hunting and was a friend of Presidents Theodore Roosevelt and Herbert Hoover.

20. **The Indian Wars** – as part of America's expansionist by European settlers, the attempted genocide, holocaust, and ethnic cleansing of the indigenous people took place from the fifteenth through nineteenth centuries. Prior to the European's arrival, there has been estimates of between nine million to eighteen million lived in the Americas. By the 1890's, that number had been reduced to about 250,000.

21. **Human Zoos** – from about the mid 1800's to the late 1950's, you could find the famous human zoos all over Europe and part of the United States. In the zoos, African Americans, Native Americans and others were caged and watched them like an animal. It was not only a crime against humanity but also crime against dignity. Unfortunately, human zoos are yet another uncomfortable example of the world's flawed past of racism and what's worse is they happen to be a part of our recent history. Racism has come a long way since the 1800s, but it still occurs today. These wildly flawed incidents of the past are horrific but should not be forgotten. Along with paying homage to those who suffered, acknowledging these acute examples of racism in our

past often reflects the issues of today that will undoubtedly shock and appall generations to come.

22. **How the Jews became White** - Jewish people eventually just assimilated just like every other European immigrant. Their identity began to get absorbed into a larger white identity. It's easy to know who's Jewish within Jewish people. But it's harder when not around Jewish people. Especially in areas where there are few Jews. Most Jews in America are of Ashkenazi (indigenous to Europe) and pretty much look exactly like Europeans (since that is their ancestry and religion). The experience of Mizrahi/Sephardi Jews is more distinct outside of a tradition "white American" identity. They are probably more assumed to be Arab. Most Jewish Americans are not of this background or have mixed in with Ashkenazis and have been absorbed into them.

23. **White Flight** - refers to white families leaving areas that have a large concentration of subordinate group members and moving into other suburban or rural communities for a variety of reasons. The result is that segregated communities seem to be evolving.

24. **Redlining and Gentrification** - redlining is a discriminatory practice and process of denying loans anywhere inside certain community boundaries based on racial or ethnic population of the community. The predominantly black neighborhood would be denied or charged more services including home loans relating to real estate companies and banks. Many neighborhoods were deemed 'high risk' with a racist assumption. The primary criteria for a neighborhood being deemed "high risk" was usually the level of minority residence, not income, and even upper class African-Americans with stable jobs, high incomes, and good neighborhoods, would find it hard, or impossible, to get a loan. Gentrification, in contrast, is based on economic depravity of a community. Gentrification brings money back into the community instead of blocking financial resources. The

controversial part of gentrification is it makes neighborhoods unsuited to poor residents. Redlining and gentrification lead to a migration of population out of the community. In the case of redlining it is white flight with the more affluent leaving whereas in gentrification it is the poor that are removed.

25. **Police Brutality** - is a violation of someone's basic civil rights. It is also a betrayal of trust and responsibility that society places in a law enforcement officer. Police officers have very broad legal powers and can cause serious harm if those powers are abused. They put their lives on the line to serve and protect the public and sometimes they have to make split second life and death decisions. While it is suspected that the majority of law enforcement officers perform their duties in a lawful manner, there are well documented instances in which some subordinate group members as a whole have different experiences with their encounters. The recent addition of technology via cameras where social media have shown instances of excessive force being used by a few officers, shootings of unarmed people when other non-lethal methods could have used and other forms of police brutality. There are countless findings documenting our country's pervasive racism today, such as that Africa Americans male teenagers' have twenty-one times the likelihood of being shot and killed by police as their counterparts.

26. **Homestead Act** - was a United States Federal law that gave an applicant freehold title to 160 acres of undeveloped land outside of the original 13 colonies. The new law required three steps: file an application, improve the land, and file for deed of title. Anyone who had never taken up arms against the U.S. Government, including freed slaves, could file an application and improvements to a local land office. The Act was signed into law by President Abraham Lincoln on May 20, 1862. Eventually 1.6 million homesteads were granted, and 270,000,000 acres were privatized between 1862 and 1988, a total of 10% of all lands in the

United States. "The act remained in effect for more than a century, and the last claim made under it was granted in 1988 for a parcel of land in Alaska."[xciv]

After slavery, freed blacks stayed in the South because they were unable to take advantage of the act due to its specific requirements that needed money and the recently freed slaves did not have enough money.

27. **Black Wall Street (Tulsa Riots)** - a town in Greenwood community of Tulsa, Oklahoma, also known as 'Black Wall Street' which was bustling with black owned businesses, hospitals, insurance companies, stores, and banks. After the Civil War, freed slaves migrated and were exiled to this community. In 1921, white mobs burn down the community due jealousy and envy after an alleged black shoe shiner was accused of assaulted a white elevator operator. They used guns and bombs, sticks of dynamite and burning balls of turpentine were dropped from planes to destroy the town's black homes and businesses. Over 300 blacks were killed, over 10,000 blacks were left homeless and their businesses were looted, damaged and destroyed. This is considered one of the worst racial violence in the history of the United States.

28. **Rosewood Massacre** - was a violent, racially motivated conflict that took place during the first week of January 1923 in rural Levy County, Florida, United States. At least six blacks and two whites were killed, and the town of Rosewood was abandoned and destroyed during what was characterized as a race riot. Racial disturbances were common during the early 20th century in the United States, reflecting the nation's rapid social changes. Florida had an especially high number of lynching in the years before the massacre, including a well-publicized incident in December 1922.

29. **Tuskegee Experiment** - for forty years between 1932 and 1972, the U.S. Public Health Service (PHS) conducted an

experiment on 399 black men in the late stages of syphilis. These men, for the most part illiterate sharecroppers from one of the poorest counties in Alabama, were never told what disease they were suffering from or of its seriousness. Informed that they were being treated for "bad blood," their doctors had no intention of curing them of syphilis at all. The data for the experiment was to be collected from autopsies of the men, and they were thus deliberately left to degenerate under the ravages of tertiary syphilis—which can include tumors, heart disease, paralysis, blindness, insanity, and death.

The fortieth-year study was controversial for reasons related to ethical standards, primarily because researchers failed to treat patients appropriately after the 1940s validation of penicillin as an effective cure for the disease. Revelation of study failures led to major changes in U.S. law and regulation on the protection of participants in clinical studies. Now studies require informed consent (with exceptions possible for U.S. Federal agencies which can be kept secret by Executive Order), communication of diagnosis, and accurate reporting of test results.

30. **Lynching** - is and was an act of terrorism. The whole purpose was and is to instill fear into the people you wish to silence or control. Racist used it to keep those whom they hated silent and under their control and make them feel superior to their victims. Between 1882 (when reliable statistics were first collected) and 1968 (when the classic forms of lynching had disappeared), 4,743 persons died of lynching, 3,446 of them black men and women. Mississippi (539 black victims, 42 white) led this grim parade of death, followed by Georgia (492, 39), Texas (352, 141), Louisiana (335, 56), and Alabama (299, 48). From 1882 to 1901, the annual number nationally usually exceeded 100; 1892 had a record 230 deaths (161 black, 69 white). Although lynching declined somewhat in the twentieth century, there were still 97 in 1908 (89 black, 8 white), 83 in the racially troubled postwar year of

1919 (76, 7, plus some 25 race riots), 30 in 1926 (23, 7), and 28 in 1933 (24, 4).[xcv]

31. **Hollywood Stereotypes** – the early cinema of African Americans had five stereotypes. They were the Coon, the Uncle Tom, the Mammy, the Tragic Mulatto, the Black Buck. During the past half century, roles for people of color have evolved and became mainstream but traces of these stereotypical characters can still be found in some Hollywood films today. Most cultures have stereotypical images. As more people of color get involved in directing and producing films and movies, less stereotypes of characters will be portrayed and will reflect the society in general.

32. **Indian Appropriations Acts** - the federal government realized that Native Americans drew strength from their tribal ties and memberships. On March 3, 1871, the Indian Appropriations Act was passed. This law ended treaty making between tribes and the federal government. Native Americans were stripped of their power and their strength because from that point on they were considered only as individuals. This increased the power and authority of the government and was one more step toward dismantling the tribal way of life for Native Americans.

33. **Immigration Act of 1924** - tightened immigration quotas based on the desirability of specific nationalities. The law was primarily aimed at further decreasing immigration of specific groups of Europeans, including Italians, Greeks, Poles, Slavs, and Eastern European Jews. The law affirmed the longstanding ban on the immigration of other non-white persons, with the exception of black African immigrants. Thus, virtually all Asians were forbidden from immigrating to America under the Act. Racism was probably a factor for some of the legislators who voted for the bill. Another prominent factor was isolationism. Since the end of WWI, a majority of American public opinion wanted to retreat from the "internationalist" policies of the Wilson administration. Additionally, the Red Scare stirred up fears of

"foreign agitators" in the form of anarchists, communists, labor unions, or anyone else the government perceived as a threat causing unrest.

34. **Sundown Towns** - are communities that for decades—formally or informally—kept out African Americans or other groups. They are so named because some marked their city limits with placards warning specific groups of people to stay away after the sun went down. This allowed maids and workmen to provide unskilled labor during the day. They came into existence in the late nineteenth century and were scattered throughout the nation, but more often were located in the northern states that were not pre-Civil War slave states. De facto sundown towns existed at least into the 1970s and there may still be towns today that try to keep people of color away.

35. **Chinese Exclusion Act** - passed by Congress in 1882, prohibited for a period of ten years the immigration of Chinese laborer into the United States. This act was both the culmination of more than a decade of agitation on the West Coast for the exclusion of the Chinese and an early sign of the coming change in the traditional U.S. philosophy of welcoming virtually all immigrants. In response to pressure from California, Congress had passed an exclusion act in 1879, but it had been vetoed by President Hayes on the ground that it abrogated rights guaranteed to the Chinese by the Burlingame Treaty of 1868. In 1880 these treaty provisions were revised to permit the United States to suspend the immigration of Chinese. The Chinese Exclusion Act was renewed in 1892 for another ten-year period, and in 1902 the suspension of Chinese immigration was made indefinite.

36. **Emmett Till** – was a major catalyst for the civil rights movement. Till's death and trial struck a spark of indignation that ignited protests around the world. It was the murder of this fourteen-year-old out-of-state visitor from Chicago that touched

off a world-wide clamor and cast the glare of a world spotlight on Mississippi's racism. Through the constant attention it received, Till's case became emblematic of the disparity of justice for blacks in the South.

37. **Vincent Chin** - was a Chinese American beaten to death in June 1982 in the United States, in the Detroit, Michigan enclave of Highland Park by Chrysler plant superintendent Ronald Ebens, with the help of his stepson, Michael Nitz. The murder generated public outrage over the lenient sentencing the two men originally received in a plea bargain, as the attack, which included blows to the head from a baseball bat, possessed many attributes consistent with hate crimes. Many of the layoffs in Detroit's auto industry, including Nitz's in 1979, had been due to the increasing market share of Japanese automakers, leading to allegations that Chinese American Vincent Chin received racially charged comments before his death. The case became a rallying point for the Asian American community, and Ebens and Nitz were put on trial for violating Chin's civil rights. Because the subsequent Federal prosecution was a result of public pressure from a coalition of many Asian ethnic organizations, Vincent Chin's murder is often considered the beginning of a pan-ethnic Asian American movement.

38. **Islamophobia** - is a new concept for some but it has been around for millennia. Some people have formed a dislike of a different culture or religion especially when its concepts are different than theirs. With the spread of Islam, it caused a great deal of tension between Islam and non-Muslims. There are several recent events in the past few decades that have triggered an increased awareness of this extremist Muslims that have provoked the recent fears. Events such as deposing the Iranian shah in 1979, the Gulf War in 1991, and the World Trade Centre bombings in 1993, and more recent events have made this relatively widespread. Islam has unfairly or fairly taken a lot of

the blame for a significant proportion of all the wars and social violence in the last fifty years for a variety of reasons and also because they have been focused in the Middle East. The rise of terrorism that threatens the U.S. and the West has been borne out of either ignorance or hatred constitute the painful reality of Islamophobia.

39. **Indian Boarding Schools (United States and Canada)** - were government sponsored schools used as a tool to assimilate and 'civilize' Native American children into the dominant European American culture. It attempted to forcibly integrate and educate children of Native American tribes into the United State culture by way of boarding schools. The children were forbidden to speak their native language or practice their traditional faiths. From the Indian's perspective, they were a conquered and captive people all across the country and at the mercy of the dominant culture. Despite the federal government requirement of force assimilation on the native Indians but not European immigrants, the Indians survived this ordeal and remnants of their culture remain.

In Canada, the total number of children forced into these schools was around 150,000. Most students endured ten months of school each year, and many were never allowed to return home at all during their "education." When these poor children were finally returned to their families, they were often branded as outsiders, having been so removed from their own culture that they became foreign to their own families.

Although most of these schools were shut down during the twentieth century, the last one remained open until 1996. In 2007, the Canadian government issued a formal apology to the First Nations people and enacted a $1.9 billion Canadian compensation package fund for victims of the program. As of 2013, $1.6 billion has been paid out to 105,548 families.[xcvi]

40. **King Philip's War** - was the single greatest calamity to occur in seventeenth century Puritan New England and is considered by many to be the deadliest war in the history of European settlement in North America in proportion to the population. In the space of little more than a year, twelve of the region's towns were destroyed and many more damaged, the colony's economy was all but ruined, and its population was decimated, losing one-tenth of all men available for military service. More than half of New England's towns were attacked by Native American warriors. King Philip's War began the development of a greater European-American identity. The Colonists' trials, without significant English government support, gave them a group identity separate and distinct from that of subjects of the king. The war ended sovereignty for Indian Nations in New England and eradicated the Wampanoag people through pandemics of smallpox, spotted fever, typhoid and measles; all caused by contact with Europeans. [xcvii]

41. **Bacon's Rebellion** - or the Virginia Rebellion was an uprising in 1676 in the Virginia Colony, led by Nathaniel Bacon. It was the first rebellion in the American Colonies in which discontented frontiersmen took part. Bacon's Rebellion was the result of discontent among backcountry farmers who had taken the law into their own hands against government corruption and oppression. Many Virginians were debtors. Borrowing on the strength of paper money was stopped by the British Government, leading to more discontent against the merchant classes. Many of the supporters of the rebellion were indentured servants and slaves, who were a majority of Virginia's population.[xcviii]

42. **American Slavery Compared to Arab, Roman and Latin American Slavery** - the key difference is that Roman, Arab and Latin American slavery had little or no racial element. The majority of slaves in the various empires were of the same nationality ethnically no different from their masters. Many slaves

were captives of war, and they came from societies that the empires considered to be less valued. On the other hand, slavery in America was racist. All slaves were African. In America, slavery and racism were in the same institution. Also, slavery in the Roman Empire (and elsewhere) it was justified by the law and by conquest. Roman slavery generally allowed you to progress upward and outward. Slavery began with agrarianism and ended with industrialism. So American slavery began with indentured servitude (contract slavery) and ended with chattel slavery (people as domesticated animal property).

43. **History of the Gun** - guns were invented by the Chinese around 900 A.D the first guns were like cannons and then evolved into hand cannon since then they have been evolved and been modified into guns we know today including the AK-47, AK-15 and mini guns. The gunpowder came before guns. The Chinese didn't fire bullets although they used to fire arrows out of large piece of bamboo using the gun powder. They also made the first cannon using a large piece of bamboo and rockets and grenades in a very crude and primitive form. In the beginning these weapons were very crude, inaccurate, with a low rate of fire and expensive and did not at once replace the other weapons. This came gradually and differently for infantry, cavalry and artillery as the technology developed to where are today presently.

44. **History of the Police** - Just about every society from the ancient period to the medieval period to early modern history has had some sort of police force whether it was called a police force to enforce the laws or in tribal environments a moral enforcement group. The first established policing groups probably came from the Roman Empire in 27 B.C. called the Vigiles. They were responsible for fighting fires and to be night watchmen, they were not technically considered soldiers since most of the men that worked in this group were taken from society (freedman or people that do not have every basic free right as others in the

society). Each patrol, or cohort was responsible for two out of the fourteen regions of the city. They were set up in a paramilitary style much like the police academies that most civilized countries have now.

45. **History of Prisons** - the earliest records of prisons come from the 1st millennia BC, located on the areas of mighty ancient civilizations of Mesopotamia and Egypt. During those times, prisons were almost always stationed in the underground dungeons where guilty or suspected criminals spent their life either awaiting death sentence, or a command to become slaves (often working as galley slaves). Exception from that rule comes from the home of modern democracy - Greece. There, prisoners were held in the poorly isolated buildings where they could often be visited by their friends and family. Primary source of their detention were not dungeons, high walls or bars, but simple wooden blocks that were attached to their feet. Ancient Roman Empire however continued to use harsher methods. Their prisons were built almost exclusively underground, with tight and claustrophobic passageways and cells. Prisoners themselves were held either in simple cells or chained to the walls, for life or for time. As slavery was accepted norm in those days, majority of prisoners that were not sentenced to death were sold as slaves or used by the Roman government as workforce. One of the most famous uses for the slaves in Roman Empire was as "gladiators". In addition to fighting in the arena (sometimes after lifetime of training in the special gladiator training houses, or Luduses), many slaves were tasked as a support workforce that enabled smoother run of the popular gladiator business. The most famous Gladiator battleground, the mighty Colosseum Arena in Rome had a slave army of 224 slaves that worked daily as a power source of the complicated network of 24 elevators that transported gladiators and their wild animal opponents from the underground dungeons to the arena floor.[xcix]

46. **History of White Suburbia** - federal housing policies didn't just deny opportunities to black residents. They subsidized and safeguarded whites-only neighborhoods. It started with the New Deal policies of President Franklin Roosevelt's administration and continued through World War II when the Federal Housing Administration (FHA) and the Veterans Administration (VA) and President Harry Truman signed the Housing Act of 1949. Despite decades of progress, African Americans living in largely white affluent suburbs still often find themselves caught between the two worlds of race and class. High economic status has afforded them considerable employment opportunities and political resources--but not necessarily neighbors, coworkers, or local candidates or office holders who share or even understand their concerns.

47. **Lincoln's Racism and Anti-racism** – if we judge people by the standards of their time and not in the twenty-first century, Lincoln would probably be considered a racist today based upon his personal views concerning the African slaves although he personally opposed slavery on a moral ground. His primary stand on slavery during the Civil War was to save and preserve the Union. As long as the Union was saved, ending slavery or keeping it in the slave holding states would be the byproduct. He also didn't feel that the African slaves were equal to and were inferior to whites, but few men believe that during the fifteenth through nineteenth centuries. Moreover, if we're going to be judged by the standards of future generations and centuries, none of us will ever measure up to their standards as the social evolution of humans continues to evolve.

48. **George Wallace, Governor of Alabama** - within a year of becoming governor, Wallace made national headlines by standing against the federal government on the issue of integration. He stood at the doors of a building at the University of Alabama, threatening to block the entrance of two black students to the

school. Facing him was then Assistant Attorney General Nicholas Katzenbach, sent by President John F. Kennedy to enforce a federal court's decision to integrate the university. Whether it was his conscience or political expediency that sparked him to ask for forgiveness will never be known. But when he reentered politics for the 1982 governor's race, he sought and won the vote of black constituents, and he worked with black leaders once elected. Citing his health, Wallace chose not to run for another term and announced his retirement in 1986.

49. **Cointelpro** - an acronym for Counter Intelligence Program was a series of covert and illegal projects conducted by the United States Federal Bureau of Investigation aimed at investigating and disrupting dissident political organizations within the United States. The FBI used covert operations from its inception; however, the formal COINTELPRO operations took place between 1956 and 1971. The FBI motivation at the time was "protecting national security, preventing violence, and maintaining the existing social and political order." Targets included groups suspected of being subversive, such as communist and socialist organizations; people suspected of building a "coalition of militant black nationalist groups" ranging from the Black Panther Party and Republic of New Africa, to "those in the non-violent civil rights movement," such as Martin Luther King, Jr. and others associated with the Southern Christian Leadership Conference, the National Association for the Advancement of Colored People (NAACP), the Congress on Racial Equality (CORE), and other civil rights groups; "White Hate Groups" including the Ku Klux Klan and National States Rights Party; a broad range of organizations lumped together under the title "New Left" groups, including Students for a Democratic Society, the National Lawyers Guild, the Weathermen, almost all groups protesting the Vietnam War, and even individual student demonstrators with no group affiliation; and a

special project seeking to undermine nationalist groups such as those "Seeking Independence for Puerto Rico." The directives governing COINTELPRO were issued by FBI Director J. Edgar Hoover, who ordered FBI agents to "expose, disrupt, misdirect, discredit, or otherwise neutralize" the activities of these movements and their leaders.[c]

50.. **Real Estate Steering** - in real estate, steering is the practice of guiding prospective residents to certain neighborhoods or away from other neighborhoods or areas based on their identity as part of a protected class such as race.

51. **School Tracking** - in a tracking system, the entire school population is assigned to classes according to whether the students' overall achievement is above average, normal, or below average. Students attend academic classes only with students whose overall academic achievement is the same as their own. The researchers found that the proportion of high-ability African American and Latino American students not taking college prep courses in math and science was more than twice that of white and Asian American students of the same ability level.

52. **Mass Incarceration of Black Men** – today's people of color continue to be disproportionately incarcerated, policed, and sentenced to death at significantly higher rates than their white counterparts. Furthermore, racial disparities in the criminal-justice system threaten communities of color—disenfranchising thousands by limiting voting rights and denying equal access to employment, housing, public benefits, and education to millions more. In light of these disparities, it is imperative that criminal-justice reform evolves as one of the Civil Rights issues of the twenty-first century.

One in every three black males born today can expect to go to prison at some point in their life, compared to one in every six Latino males, and one in every 17 white males, if current incarceration trends continue.[ci]

A criminal-justice reform agenda that included everything from calls for a close and hard look at what sends people to jail, which crimes and which defendants get the longest sentences, the use of solitary confinement and the loss of voting rights after release.

53. **Boston School Busing Riots** - it wasn't until the mid-1970s that Boston's "busing crisis" finally garnered national attention. It was easy to forget that this wasn't a new phenomenon, that black people in Boston and other cities had been fighting for years to secure equal education, and that powerful local officials and national politicians underwrote school segregation in the North. School desegregation was about the constitutional rights of black students, but in Boston and other Northern cities, the story has been told and retold as a story about the feelings and opinions of white people. The mass protests and violent resistance that greeted school desegregation in mid-1970s Boston engraved that city's "busing crisis" into school textbooks and cemented the failure of busing and school desegregation in the popular imagination. Contemporary news coverage and historical accounts of Boston's school desegregation have emphasized the anger that white people in South Boston felt and have rendered Batson and other black Bostonians as bit players in their own civil-rights struggle.[cii]

54. **Man Made Ebola and A.I.D.S.** – there is an ongoing debate as to whether AIDS and Ebola viruses did not originate from monkeys left alone in the wild or they were bioengineered in American laboratories. There have been numerous conspiracy theories over the years from a variety of sources, so the verdict is still out on this subject.

55. **Black Churches Bombings and Fires** - Black churches have suffered at the hands of thugs and terrorists throughout the Civil Rights era, as they had for a century before, but such attacks aren't a matter of remote history. As recently as the 1990s, a wave of fire-bombings hit black churches.

56. **Church Shootings** - the Center for Homicide Research produced a study_using online newspaper archive articles to document all cases of shootings on church property within the United States from 1980 to 2005. According to the data, there was a total of 139 shootings on church property with a total death toll of 185 people. During that 25-year period there were an average of six shootings on church property every year.[ciii]

57. **How the Irish and Italians Became White** - the Italians and Irish as immigrants have integrated into the American society over several generations. They assimilated into the American lifestyle much easier than Africans because their genetic makeups were not as obvious. They basically blended into white America and were accepted by dominant culture and became Americanized. On the other hand, Africans can't blend in so easily into a white American society due to their inherited distinctive physical characteristics.

58. **The Perpetuation of the Idea of the "Model Minority" and Elite Upbringing** - elite education and proper upbringing will get you only so far in the dominant culture. Unfortunately, it is still naïve in the twenty-first century to think that elite upbringing can insulate subordinate members or their children from racism. No matter who subordinate members are, how they carry themselves or how much wealth they have accumulated, it means nothing because when they 'walk' into the door, the color of their skin tone is the first thing some members of the dominant culture see. There will then be assumptions made about them. Then they will have to prove that they belong until they are accepted. Every immigrant that came here from other countries was mistreated by dominant culture, but their skin tone always prevailed. They were eventually accepted but those with a darker skin tone will have a much difficult time to be accepted in society. Parents of children from subordinate groups need to have the 'talk' with their children and teach them the facts of the real world so they can be

able to deal with them. Otherwise, they won't be in a state of shock when the realities set in.

59. **Housing Discrimination** - is discrimination in which an individual or family is treated unequally when trying to buy, rent, lease, sell or finance a home based on certain characteristics, such as race, class, sex, religion, national origin, and familial status. This type of discrimination can lead to housing and spatial inequality and racial segregation which, in turn, can exacerbate wealth disparities between certain groups. In the United States, housing discrimination began after the abolition of slavery as part of a federally sponsored law, but has since been made illegal; however, studies show that housing discrimination still exists.[civ]

60. **Systematic Placement of Highways and Building Projects to Create Ghettos** - the subordinate group's inability to lobby, legislate in generally poorer, minority communities in US cities led to a lot of them getting razed in the name of eminent domain and the interstate system. With the razing and moving of entire communities, it displaced, and, especially during the great white flight of the 50's, 60's and 70's (and 80's, caused massive exoduses, displacement, and loss of culture, identity, and fair housing for minorities.

61. **Medical Experimentation on Poor People of Color Especially Blacks Including Surgical and Gynecological Experimentation** – there is a long and shameful history of medical research and experimentation on African Americans in the United States (often against the will and/or knowledge of the test subjects), from slavery to the present day. The medical experimentation on blacks is not an aberration that peaked during the infamous Tuskegee syphilis experiments, but rather has been so common in U.S. history that blacks are justifiably suspicious of doctors and hospitals today. From experimental surgeries on slaves without anesthesia during antebellum America to experiments by the CIA using infectious mosquitos to test

110

biological warfare technology on black neighborhoods as recently as the 1950s to the 1970s, there is a shocking history of the medical dehumanization of African Americans.

A study from Proceedings of the National Academy of Sciences states white doctors believe Black patients have tougher skin, feel less pain and other ridiculously false notions. If you are Black and enter an emergency room, you are 22% more likely to receive less pain medicine than whites which also explains the longer wait times compared to other groups. New studies indicate young white doctors treat Black people like something other than human. Not even Black children are safe. If a Black child shows up at the emergency room with appendicitis, which requires surgery, they're 80% less likely to receive opioids. There is some hope though. A study from the American Journal of Gastroenterology says that Blacks can receive better medical care if we go to more diverse hospitals. But, the problem is there aren't enough studies. More Africa Americans doctors are needed to service patients on the lower end of society's racial social order.[cv]

62. **History of Planned Parenthood** - although planned Parenthood supporters will just say that the founder, Margaret Sanger's views don't represent the organization today, if you look at where the clinics are that do abortions, a disproportionate number of them are in or near African American communities. The Negro Project was initiated in 1939 by Margaret Sanger, founder of Planned Parenthood. It was a collaborative effort between the American Birth Control League and Sanger's Birth Control Clinical Research Bureau. For eugenics, it wasn't controversial, it was integral to the implementation of eugenics to eliminate the 'unfit'.

63. **Forced Sterilization** - inevitably, eugenics requires that someone decide who is fit to reproduce and who isn't, and every someone has values and an agenda related to their own interests, not the interest of the species. Even those who profess to have

humanity's progress are operating according on a set of cultural values, which are always narrow minded and shortsighted in some sense. In many cases, the choice to breed or not can be voluntary. However, if sterilization is forced and getting rid of some so-called society's undesirables by the dominant culture group become a major issue with a racial or sexual connotation. The genocide of racial groups can also come into play and be a consideration.

64. **Cutting children Out of Pregnant Black Mothers as Part of Lynching** - Mary Turner and her unborn child was lynched May 19, 1918 by a mob in Lowndes County, Georgia. Today a historical marker bears the spot of the heinous incident. Smith's murder was followed by a week-long mob-driven manhunt in which at least 13 people were killed. Among those killed was Mary's husband, Hayes Turner, who was seized from custody after his arrest on the morning of May 18, 1918, and Lynched. The murders of Hayes and Mary Turner caused a brief national outcry. Following the lynching, more black residents fled the area, despite threats against the lives of anyone who tried to leave.

65. **Eurocentric Beauty Standard Falsification** - one manifestation of the dominant culture group is the use of whiteness as the standard of beauty. When whiteness is considered superior, white people are considered more attractive by definition and, insofar as the appearance of people of other races deviates from that standard, they are considered not as attractive. African American women have had to change their natural physical appearances in some work places and schools by using harmful and chemical products to straighten the hair or wear wigs or weaves because it doesn't comply with the dominant culture's identity. This has resulted in a billion-dollar hair industry worldwide. Over a time period, this beauty standard may change due to shifting demographics and the intermixing of the racial groups.

66. **Erasure and Eradication of all Achievements of Ancient Africa and Kemet** - the Kemites' contribution to history is much more sinister. While Europe and the rest of the West readily credit ancient Greece as its foundation, this credit isn't extended to Africa. At a time when Western society was building itself on the labor of black African slaves, white Europeans were hardly in a position to credit their slaves' ancestors with providing the foundation of that very same society. Since the Kemites have been all but excluded from history, one can't help but wonder if another culture has been kept even more in the dark. A tantalizing question emerges: Did the Kemites, like the Greeks, draw their knowledge from another source as well?

67. **White Washing of History and Cultural Practices of People of Color** - whitewashing refers to the tendency of members of the dominant group to define subordinate groups members in the context and standards of the dominant culture based on its experiences and worldviews.

68. **Media Manipulation and Bias** - racial bias of any sort has an impact, whether inferred, spoken, or covertly suggested. People don't always analyze issues when presented to them in writing, social media, on air, or on television on a regular basis. Any biases done succinctly and repeatedly, installs itself into the minds and thought processes of subordinate group members, and register there. Racial bias against certain racial group members, whether true or not, begins to take root with opinions formed, ideas exchanged, and subsequent actions taken. Whether these biases are acted upon immediately, or stored, and aired at a later date, sometimes impacts the subordinate group member blindly, and unjustly. They become ingrained in the thought process in his life, work, social connections.

69. **Perpetuation of the Myth of Reverse Racism -** reverse racism is a highly controversial form of racism against the dominant group culture that refers to several ideas. The current

occurrence of reverse racism in the United States (where the term originated and is primarily used) is highly disputed. In the United States, many people criticize policies such as affirmative action as an example of reverse racism and claim that it is systemic racially-based discrimination. Supporters argue that affirmative action policies counteract the systemic and cultural racism against minorities by providing a balancing force, and that affirmative action does not qualify as racist because the policies are enacted by politicians (who are mostly part of the dominant culture in the United States) and directed towards their own racial group.

Reverse racism is a term often applied to blacks being prejudice against dominant group members although a strong argument can be made that is a no such thing as reverse racism. There is the belief that racism only flows in one direction. Racism is also defined as having prejudicial views that is enacted with power. It means that in order for reverse racism to exist, a racial group can have prejudicial views, discriminatory feelings and sediments, however, it also must have cultural racism and power. Examples would include controlling the distribution of wealth among a nation, its educational opportunities, employment opportunities and room for professional growth and what images are portrayed in the media of the subordinate or oppressed groups. Racism is considered to be a system of social power. It is the belief that subordinate group members do not possess such power, therefore, they cannot be racist. They can, however, be prejudice and discriminatory but not racist as racism requires power.

70. **Access to Voting and Voting Suppression** - access to voting that has eroded public trust in the system is a hotly debated issue in the United States. It has a dipropionate impact on people of color and women including African-Americans, Latinos, Native Americans, Asian-Americans and Pacific Islanders, and LGBTQ individuals, particularly transgender people. There are specific hurdles they are most likely to encounter at the ballot box. The

trend began after the GOP wave of 2010 and picked up steam after the Supreme Court's 2013 decision that gutted major provisions of the Voting Rights Act. The laws typically impose strict identification requirements at the ballot box or limiting early and absentee voting. Examples of restrictive voting measures in some states include providing a form of identification for Native Americans to include legal name, current street address but many live on reservations that lack street addresses and instead use P.O. boxes. Some states have early voting restrictions, voter ID laws, registrations placed on hold because minor mismatches on documents like their driver's licenses violate the state's new "exact match" requirement.

The legal battles over restrictive voting measures exist in several states involving both major political parties in preventing voter fraud, arcane voting laws, advocating the expansions of voting access, including automatic voter registration that are done to stop the suppression the voter efforts. Both parties have vested political interest where one party have advocated the expansion of voting efforts and the other party trying to restrict them.

71. **White Fragility** - is basically the state in which whites find racial tension and stress to be overwhelming. Since whites do not have to think about their skin color on a day to day basis the way that nonwhites do, it's easier for whites to become defensive, irritated, annoyed, angry as well as resentful over racial stress. Many whites refuse to talk honestly and fairly about the subject because it means they will have to look at the root cause of why there is such a divide between whites and nonwhites and have to forgo pointing to graphs and charts to explain their views.

72. **White on White Crime and White on Everybody Else Crime** - there is a tendency in every racial group to regard crimes committed against them by other racial groups as more heinous than the same crimes committed within the group. There is an understanding that is in relations to media stories about black-on-

black crime is a red herring to change the conversation away from crimes committed by whites against disempowered ones. Despite the lack of media attention given to white-on-white crime, we should not be ignorant of what is taking place across the nation. What is happening in the black community is happening in the white community as well. The majority of homicides that occur are intra-racial, or between members of the same race. However, in the media, there has been heavy focus on just one group committing these crimes. Black-on-black crime has saturated media coverage in recent years, but no one is talking about the high rate of white-on-white crime. The media is purposely denying these facts, even though the violence has reached an alarming rate in some areas.

73. **Irish Slavery, Jewish Slavery, African Slavery, Native American Slavery** - oppression has existed in every culture since the beginning of humankind. There are certain racial groups that oppress others, and when they do, they subject those people to derogatory acts that shame them. Each country writes their own history books the way they want their people to read them. The average American takes this for face value, never question or attempt to delve deeper into history. That is why they do not know about any other types of oppression or slavery other than the slavery of Africans brought to the Americas. The fact still remains, however, that if any or all of these groups are overshadowed, it's because it was the way the history books were written. The history books and classes are mostly glossing over the true horrors of our history.

This does not mean the Irish, Jews, Native American or Chinese didn't suffer. Many were forced to leave to seek a better life and were often indentured servants. They were mistreated. But they had an ending period and were able to pursuit their life's goal at some point. The Africans were slaves for life. The stories of other type of slavery should also be told but there are differences.

Telling the stories about African slaves should not diminish the stories of others. Whether or not the African slaves suffered more or less than other immigrant is one thing, but the fact remains that they suffered tremendously. Africans were the only racial group taken from their country by force. All other were allowed to remain in their homeland and fight for freedom but African slaves were not. And then they were made to feel worthless and degrading in their new country. African's never got the chance to be immigrants. Chinese, Jewish and Irish immigrants chose to come to America and weren't slaves.

The Irish and the Jews suffered but they were never kidnapped from their homeland, taken in coffin sized holds, and sold on an auction block to people who treated them like animals. The Irish, Jews and Indians were never formally forced into formal slavery as Africans brought here. Slavery is an entirely unique brand of injury, different from beatings, or having to live in poverty. Even well treated slaves were still not free, subject to someone else's will and were also beaten, raped, worked to death, mutilated, and suffered all sorts of physical injuries. I'm sure the other groups suffered some non-corporal injuries as well but as a group, they weren't forced into it.

Living conditions and poverty were the major issues among those immigrants. But they still had civil rights even if they were limited. Africans were brought to the country and forced to stay and work against their will. They weren't compensated for their work and had no human rights. They couldn't make a better life for themselves and their families through better employment opportunities because they were slaves.

The native Americans and indigenous people are in a different category. A look into post-Colonialism and you'll see that Europeans have been degrading indigenous populations all over the world. That's more of a cultural/social issue than one of slavery. Indigenous people also suffered genocide in the Americas, Australia, Asia, Australia and New Zealand.

74. **White Police Officers Murdering Unarmed Men, Women, and Children and not Being Convicted -** Bowling Green State University's Police Integrity Lost project shows that only 29 officers have been convicted for killing on duty since 2005, mostly on lesser charges. Police are 33 percent less likely than a regular citizen to be convicted of a crime, and the conviction rate for cops charged with some form of murder is 35 percent—half that of the normal population. In fact, in the last 13 years, only one officer has been convicted of intentional murder. And in the rare case in which a cop is convicted, the officer hardly ever does time for killing a black man. Between 2005 and 2017, 33 of the 49 people killed by indicted cops were black, but only five officers were convicted, making the homicide conviction rate for black victims a mere 12 percent.

75. **Population Control Warfare Worldwide** - restrained worldwide population growth should be considered a very important issue in our complex physical, ecological, biocultural, and sociopolitical landscape. Regulating human population size and confronting the numerous problems that will be engendered by its eventual and inevitable contraction, should thus be accorded a central position within the modern dilemma, and as such should be dealt with much more forthrightly, and promptly, than has been the case. Education and offering birth control methods are the best ways, especially in developing countries. Women who are better educated have more economic opportunities and are less likely to want a large family. This is especially true when they have easy access to birth control so that they can more easily prevent a pregnancy from happening in the first place. This is apparent when you look at population growth in developed countries where women are well-educated and have

easy access to birth control. Population growth in developed countries is very slow, usually at less than 1% per year.

76. **Chemtrails** - there is a spectrum of misinformation when it comes to the topic of airplane exhaust. On one side, you have the people who believe there is a nefarious plot to poison the globe with toxic metals, bacteria, viral materials, etc. On the other hand, some people trust and believe everything they hear from authority. These people claim that the trails are nothing more than water vapor, aside from a small amount of carbon dioxide. As with any debate like this, the truth lies somewhere in the middle.

77. **Oil Spills and Chemical Dumping in Oceans Worldwide** - occurs when harmful substances—often chemicals or microorganisms—contaminate a stream, river, lake, ocean, aquifer, or other body of water, degrading water quality and rendering it toxic to humans or the environment. Petroleum is another form of chemical pollutant that usually contaminates water through oil spills when a ship rupture. Oil spills usually have only a localized effect on wildlife but can spread for miles. The oil can cause the death of many fish and stick to the feathers of seabirds causing them to lose the ability to fly. Every man made chemical ever manufactured and the combination of organo-chemicals which produced unknown chemicals when they combined. Very few insecticides and herbicides are not pollutants and likely all fresh water sources as well as the oceans are inundated with them. Also, solvents, oil, cleaning products, plastics, metals, heavy metals, PCBs, sewage, mercury, radiated debris, and radioactive materials have probably been dumped in the ocean.

78. **Water Fracking** - the process of drilling down into the earth before a high-pressure water mixture is directed at the rock to release the gas inside is called fracking. Water, sand and chemicals are injected into the rock at high pressure which allows the gas to flow out to the head of the well. Hydraulic fracturing,

hydrofracking or "fracking" is a new technology used by the energy industry to unlock previously inaccessible supplies of domestic oil and clean-burning natural gas. This "shale" oil and gas, up to a few years ago, was thought to be impossible to recover. But over the past few years fracking, along with horizontal drilling has unlocked this abundant resource. Water Fracking is being debated as far the process contributing to contaminated groundwater polluting the water source as well as a cause of earthquakes. There are arguments on both sides, but a definitive answer is inconclusive.

79. **GMO Foods Worldwide and Monsanto** – the ongoing debate on the consumption of genetically modifying food items has not reached any definite conclusion. There are mixed responses on both sides of the argument. Humans have been genetically modifying crops for a long time. So, on a fundamental level it shouldn't make much difference. However, the outcome of the studies of these organisms have been interpreted differently depending on one point of view. More studies may need to determine if the protein structures of plants modify their effects on humans. There is some evidence that hybridization of wheat after the 1940's may have greatly increased the incidence of celiac disease. Also, what people are really concerned about are GMO organisms marketed by Monsanto to be resistant to their herbicide Round-up.

80. **Affirmative action** - has been a very controversial and hotly contested subject in a quest to address past inequalities and injustices for those subordinate groups at the bottom of the world's social racial order. In 1995, the United States Supreme Court and the European Court of Justice delivered landmark rulings on affirmative action laws. They issued a world-wide debate on race and gender-based equality and the philosophy underpinning them that also impacted the continent of Australia and other countries.

The United States was a largely segregated society for a century after slavery and the Civil War. The South operated under Jim Crow laws until the 1960's. All the America institutions from economic, law, labor, criminal justice system, education, sex and war was controlled by the dominant culture in which black and brown people were not part of the process. Institutions such as Historical Black Colleges and Universities, black fraternities and sororities, the NAACP, black churches, black radio stations and others were created.

Affirmative action only became an issue when the recipients were members of the lower end of society's racial social order. African Americans weren't allowed access to the GI bill in the 1940's after World War II. Ninety-eight percent of all Federal Housing Administration (FHA) loans were given to whites. It is widely known that most of the generational wealth is tied to home and business ownership. Millions of acres of free land were given to the European settlers in the South where the Indian Removal Act of 1824 created the Tears of Trails and opened land for cultivation in the Midwest and the West opened land.

This created s tremendous economic base and head start for whites that subordinate groups were not a part of. After the slaves were freed from bondage with the signing of the Emancipation Proclamation in 1863, they were given no land or resources to transition themselves into society.

Thus, a society that channels resources toward the dominant group at the expense of the subordinate groups, then the fact that the dominant group members are considered more qualified is in of itself unfair. No one questions why a dominant group member got the great job or accepted in a prestigious university. It is assumed they were just highly qualified and based on merit, not because a certain quota had to filled.

Furthermore, the fact that dominant group members appear to be more qualified than the subordinate group members may be the result of racism based on the previous distribution of resources. Likewise, a society that implement public policies through its political discourse that disproportionately impacts subordinate racial groups when the mechanism of the disparate impact is disputable.

81. **Environmental Justice** - refers to inequitable environmental burdens borne by groups such as racial minorities, women, residents of economically disadvantaged areas, or residents of developing nations. Historically, undesirable things such as waste dumps, nuclear power, etc. have been placed in poorer communities, mostly in minority communities which most of the people are powerless in society. Nobody wants a waste dump in their backyard and of course the powerful in society will determine the locations where the dumps go which usually are near underprivileged communities. In many cases, they produce pollutions that sometimes contaminate the surrounding waterways, air and in many cases, create a high density of cancer in the area.

Environmental justice proponents generally seek to redress inequitable distributions of environmental burdens (pollution, industrial facilities, crime, etc.) and equitably distribute access to environmental goods such as nutritious food, clean air & water, parks, recreation, health care, education, transportation, safe jobs, etc. Self-determination and participation in decision-making are key components of environmental justice. Some of the root causes of environmental injustices include institutionalized racism, unresponsive or unaccountable government policies and regulation; and lack of resources and power in affected communities.

82. **Elaine, Arkansas Race Massacre of 1919** - the Red Summer refers to the summer and fall of 1919, in which race riots exploded in a number of cities in both the North and South. The three most

violent episodes occurred in Chicago, Washington, D.C., and Elaine, Arkansas.

The Elaine Massacre was by far the deadliest racial confrontation in Arkansas history and possibly the bloodiest racial conflict in the history of the United States. From October 1-3, 1919, a race war exploded in Phillips County, Arkansas. On the night of September 30, a small group of black men and women were gathering a rural church to organize a sharecroppers' and tenant farmers' union -- the Progressive Farmers and Household Union of America. When two white law-enforcement officers arrived at the church, one later claiming they were looking for a bootlegger, shots were exchanged. One white officer was killed and the other wounded. As word of the shootings spread throughout the county, the local sheriff sent out a call for men including a call to Mississippi to come to the aid of white men in Phillips County. Hundreds of armed men jumped into trains, trucks, and cars and, crossing into Arkansas, fired out of windows at every black person they saw. There were 500 to 1000 more white men with guns, shooting and killing women and children.

Soldiers from the United States Army eventually restored order, although some claimed the military participated in the killings. By the time the shooting ended, 25 blacks and five whites were listed as officially dead. Many blacks believed that perhaps as many as 237 were killed, their bodies dumped in the Mississippi River or left to rot in the canebrake. The white establishment charged that blacks had formed a secret conspiracy to rise up and overthrow the white planters, take their land and rape their women. cvi

No evidence was ever produced to substantiate the charge. In all, 77 black citizens — and no whites — were tried and sentenced for their alleged role in the riot. Twelve men sentenced to death received legal assistance and were eventually released from prison.

83. Stolen Inventions, Culture Concepts and Blueprints from African People and Other Indigenous People Worldwide - there have been many great civilizations in Africa from the Egyptians, Ethiopians, Ghana and Songhai Empires to the Kingdom of Zimbabwe. No civilization can exist without technological innovation. Africa has not been at the forefront of science and technology in the last few centuries due to the European Colonialism in Africa and propaganda that has not highlighted those achievements. The invention of mathematics is placed firmly in Africa. 'The oldest known possibly mathematical object is the Lebombo bone, discovered in the Lebombo mountains of Swaziland. Swaziland was also the first place that mining and smelting of minerals took place. Ethiopia was the first country to establish laws. Ethiopians also established international trade. Africans sailed to South America and Asia hundreds of years before the Europeans. Several ancient African cultures birthed discoveries in astronomy. Many of these are foundations on which we still rely, and some were so advanced that their mode of discovery still cannot be understood. The Dogon people of Mali amassed a wealth of detailed astronomical observations.

Other inventions from African Americans include the global positioning system (GPS), Cardio pad, CAT scan, cyber tracker and cellular antenna technology Surgery Robot, ultraviolet camera/spectrograph, dry cleaning or 'dry scouring', Laserphaco Probe for laser cataract surgery and treatment for glaucoma, multi-core processor, digital laser and 3D Printer and movie graphics, traffic light, ironing board, automatic gear shift, ice cream scoop, sprinklers, dust pan and brush, modern elevator (automatic doors), cloth dryer, railroad crossing signal, carbon-filament light bulb , home security system, gas heating furnace, modern day fireproof safe, protective mailbox design, affordable shoes (automatic shoemaking machine), portable cardiograms, modern and mobile refrigerator, microphones, touchtone phones, potato chips, pacemaker, peanut butter, video gaming console, blood plasma and blood bank, safer cataract remover, gas mask, squeeze mop, modern lawn mower (rotary blade), automatic oil cup for train's axels and bearings, the hot comb among many others.

The indigenous people have also been responsible for inventions involving food, dental and medical care. The Aztec Indians sticks to brush their teeth and salt and charcoal were used to clean the teeth. They developed supplicated medical tools and cures for diseases such and scurvy among others. They also were instrumental in many food products such as many different types of potatoes in which French fries and mashed potatoes are made. Other food products include vanilla, barbecue Sause, gum and chocolate.

The dominant culture sometimes steals from the subordinate racial groups that they conquer and do not give them proper credit for their contributions That is a cultural theft. When this happens, they not only steal from the person who made the contribution but also from the culture of the subordinate racial group. The stealing of cultural artifacts and the subsequent lies in the history books are problematic for future generations who are not told the truth and it also devalues the subordinate racial group's contributions in society. For example, Thomas Edison was credited for invented the light bulb among other things, however, it was later learned that most of those things were invented by Nikolai Tesla, an African America. Nonetheless, the scientific principles of those inventions remained true even though the named changed (Tesla later got his credit). When this happens, the future generations are manipulated in the history books.

Likewise, on its 150th anniversary, Jack Daniels, the Tennessee whiskey distillery conceded that its official history didn't tell the whole story of its origins. It credited an African American named Nearis Green, a former slave along with other enslaved men, for their contributions in the whiskey making process that they learned in Africa. It is encouraging to see a heightened awareness of the hidden racial politics behind some of America's heritages.

84. **Blockbusting** - the practice of persuading white homeowners to sell quickly and usually at a loss by appealing to the fear that minority groups and especially Black people will move into the neighborhood, causing property values to decline. The property is then resold at inflated prices.

85. **Mass murders and massacres worldwide** - the vast bulk of violent crime (in any country) is committed by men. Most mass shootings in the US are committed by white men because there are more white men (63% of male population, 64% of shooters) than nonwhite men. However, black men (13% of male population, 16% of shooters) and especially Asian men (5% of male population, 9% of shooters) are over-represented, while Latino (17% of male population, almost zero shootings) are hardly represented at all.[cvii]

86. **Racial Steering** - refers to the practice in which real estate brokers guide prospective home buyers towards or away from certain neighborhoods based on their race. It can also be based on religion, sex, or age.

87. **Flint Michigan Water Poisoning Crisis** - began in 2014 when a state-appointed emergency manager decided to save money by switching Flint's water supply from Lake Huron (which they were paying the city of Detroit for), to the Flint River that runs through town known to locals for its filth. The corrosive water caused lead to leach from old pipes. Flint returned to the Detroit system in October 2015 after elevated lead levels were discovered in children. Lead poisoning is irreversible, and some Pediatricians fear the Flint children who tested with elevated levels will suffer lifelong consequences. The city of Flint, Michigan has suffered greatly during the past three decades. General Motors closed down their plants in the city which caused many socioeconomics issues due

to job losses. Forty percent of the citizens were unemployed, and fifteen percent of the houses are boarded up.

88. **The Devils Punch Bowl - Natchez Mississippi -** is a place located in Natchez, Mississippi where during the Civil War, authorities forced tens of thousands of freed slaves to live into concentration camps. The Devil's Punchbowl was a Union run encampment, and there were others set up around the South. The South was not permitted to have such camps because they were of a martial/military order. These existed at the end of the war to basically provide forts for Yankee encampments but the one in Natchez was nothing short of an "Extermination Camp. [cviii]

The Newly freed slaves would make their way to these camps as a stop over to travel further up river in hopes of building lives for themselves. The old southern plantations were broke, they could not sustain their own families, much less a huge population of freed slaves, so the newly freed slaves, sought out the Yankee camps. But these camps became "Extermination" camps, hard labor and sickness ram rampant in the Devils Punchbowl. The population explored from about 10,000 to 12,000 rapidly after the newly freed slaves reached the camp. The Union army built an encampment wall that was sealed in and they would let them leave. Those that did escape were re-captured and the freed black men had to perform hard labor. The women and children were left to die. Smallpox and other disease broke out among the former slaves and thousands of them died. It is estimated that 20,000 freed slaves died in America concentration camp.[cix]

89. **Illegal Annexation of Hawaii** – this has been an ongoing debate even to this day as whether the United States government illegally annexed Hawaii. During the fifteen through the nineteen centuries, powerful imperialistic countries in Europe and America was colonizing territories and countries around the world. It depends upon one perspective of how the events unfolded during

the time. Some who claim that the annex was illegal base their views that in 1898 the U.S Congress annexed Hawaii by passing a joint resolution in 1898. The U.S Congress has no extraterritorial power. You need a treaty to annex foreign territory. Both parties need to come into an agreement. There were two attempts of a treaty which failed. The first treaty in 1893 was taken away by President Grover Cleveland to investigate the matter involving U.S Officials and U.S troops.

The Blount Report covers that history and the ones who were involved in the illegal overthrow committed a crime called treason. President Cleveland called upon Congress to help resolve the matter, but they refused. The second treaty in 1897 was sent by the Provisional government who were ruling Hawaii unconstitutionally. The treaty was signed by President McKinley but did not obtain the 2/3 majority vote. But still U.S Congress passed an American law to take Hawaii, kidnapped its nationals and treated them as if we were adopted. They claim there was no treaty of annexation or secession needed.

90. **School Segregation** - legal segregation between blacks and white which also included Latinos and Asians in the school create the Unanimous 1954 decision of Brown v. Board of Education. It desegregated all schools, stating that "separate educational facilities are inherently unequal." This overruled the 1896 decision of Plessy v. Ferguson, that legalized segregation. Racial segregation in schools has recent increased largely because federal courts have allowed cities and states to abandon mandatory busing and other desegregation efforts imposed in the 1960s. In 2007, a sharply divided Supreme Court ruled that public schools could no longer pursue integration strategies based explicitly on race. Yet the legal sanctioning of segregation also paved the way for white families to justify self-selecting out of what were fast becoming inferior schools in communities of color, an inferiority further fed by white flight.

91. The Conversion to Christianity – when some people enter a new culture which may be more dominant and different than their previous one, they leave their comfort zone and start to question their own traditions and beliefs and end up asking which religion is right for them. Those that convert to a religion usually do it for social or personal reasons. Some may be having some challenging times in their lives and need a source of comfort. Some people get it indoctrinated into them as kids before than have a chance to speak for themselves. Or in the case of the African slaves or indigenous people in the Americas, Australia and New Zealand or through worldwide colonization, Christianity was either forced on them through propaganda or integrated education.

Religious institutions have not been untouched by racism. "The Anglican Society for the Propagation of the Gospel in Foreign Parts owned many slaves in the Caribbean. Many combined a misapplication of the Old Testament with a mixture of racist and 'God cursed' views regarding African people. These views seem to be held by the early British Christian settlers of the New World.

Reformed Christians recognize that there is a link between Old Testament Israel and the Church (both being God's chosen people). It seems as though Christians at the time of the Transatlantic Slave Trade took this too far. They assumed instead that Christendom was the new Israel and therefore that they could treat pagan people in the same way Israel had done in the Old Testament. As God's chosen people, they believed that they had the right to enslave 'inferior' nations. This also meant that, like the Israelites, fellow Christians were not to sell each other as slaves to pagan nations, and this seems to have been the practice in Britain and much of Europe from the time of William the Conqueror. These views can be seen especially clearly in the attitudes and practices of the founding Puritan Fathers of the New World. If these views are characteristics of the general Christian attitudes of the time then this could help to explain why there was so little moral opposition in Britain to the Transatlantic Slave Trade, and why some Christians kept slaves.

Many Christians at the time were firmly opposed to the forced enslavement and ill treatment involved in the Transatlantic Slave Trade, and the Old Testament does allow a form of regulated slavery which the New Testament does not nullify. However, their application of the Old Testament does seem to be flawed and their views towards Africans racist. If this was the majority view then it does help to explain why Britain morally justified itself in the slave trade and the lack of public opposition."[cx]

A number of Christian denominations have apologized for discriminating against people of color by supporting Jim Crow and backing slavery. The United Methodist Church and the Southern Baptist Convention are some of the Christian organizations that have apologized for perpetuating racism in recent years.

Many churches have not only apologized for alienating minority groups such as blacks but have also attempted to make their churches more diverse and appoint people of color in key roles. Despite these efforts, churches in the U.S. remain largely racially segregated.[cxi]

92. **Auto Segregation** – a socialization where culturally likeminded people who have enjoyed the freedom to come together and build out a place that accommodates their specific culture more than they would be able to in a mixed neighborhood, where they would be competing with other cultures for space and expression. They are not unfriendly to outsiders. Some seek understanding and clear communication in their relationships.

93. **Separate but Equal** - for many years, racial segregation was legal in the United States under the "separate but equal" doctrine upheld by the Supreme Court in the 1896 case of Plessy v.

Ferguson. In many places, white Americans and black Americans were not allowed to ride in the same railway cars, drink from the same water fountains, attend the same schools, etc. The theory was that as long as equal facilities were provided for both groups, it was not unconstitutional to keep the groups apart. In reality, the facilities provided for black Americans were often far from equal to those provided for their white fellow citizens. In the 1950s, the Supreme Court finally rejected the "separate but equal" doctrine, ruling that racially segregated facilities were inherently unequal and thus impermissible under the Constitution's promise of "equal protection" for all citizens.

94. **Income Equality** - according to a study published by Demos in 2015, the median income for whites in 2011 was around 50% higher than it was blacks and Latinos, but white median households' wealth was around 16 times greater. It's common knowledge that in America most members of subordinate groups do not share the same wealth or opportunities to establish prosperity as their dominant group counterparts. In fact, subordinate group members in this country are paid average salaries of only 67% and 64%, respectively, of a member of a dominant group working in the same position.

95. **Poverty** - presently in America, whites make up 42% of the poor in this country but are receiving 69% of all government benefits. African Americans make up 22% of the poor population and only receives 14% of government assistance. Hispanics and Asians make up the remaining 17% of government assistance. Whites are taking 27% more of the benefits then their poor population of 42% while Africa Americans are 22% of the poor population and taking 14% which is 8% of their poor population. This just points out the faulty information and stereotypes that have emerged over the years accusing only African Americans of living off the government.

96. **Bantustan – South Africa** - Bantustans, also called black homelands or Bantu homelands, territories in South Africa from the 1950s until 1994 that were designated for the majority black population as part of the system of apartheid, the practice of separation of the races. In the 1950s the government of South Africa divided its black population according to ethnic groups or tribes and assigned them to separate regions which the government considered to be ethnic homelands. The terms Bantustan or Bantu homeland originated from the fact that the different languages of these groups are all considered to be Bantu languages

97. **Education Act – South Africa** - under the Bantu Education Act, black Africans could only access a far inferior education as compared to other racial groups. In 1979, the government allowed for black Africans to attend private schools (usually mission schools) to teach the same curriculum as white schools. This was largely a result of Catholic mission schools refusing to teach black pupils anything else. Despite the fact that these mission schools tried as best they could to minimize fees, the vast majority of black Africans could not afford to send their children to these schools. As such, most black children attended public schools and hence received an inferior education under apartheid. The Bantu Education Act was repealed in 1989.

98. **Group Areas Act – South Africa** - -Black South Africans were denied the right to live in areas of their choice until 1990, when the Group Areas Act was repealed. They could only live in areas designated for blacks; namely, townships in urban areas and Bantustans in rural areas. These areas were typically dilapidated and poorly serviced.

99. **Pass Laws – South Africa** – a further measure by government to curb labor mobility was facilitated by the implementation of the Natives (Abolition of Passes and Co-ordination of Documents) Act. The Act prescribed the

introduction of the reference book bearing photographs, details of place of origin, employment record, tax payments, fingerprints and encounters with the police. Africans were expected to carry passes with them wherever they went. Failure to produce a pass on request by the police officer was an offence. Africans could not leave the rural area for an urban one without a permit granted by the local authorities. Upon arrival in the urban area a permit to seek employment had to be obtained within 72 hours. After realizing the significant role played by the workers in industry, the government extended this system to women. For the first time in the history of South Africa, women had to carry passes. This provision resulted in a widespread strike by women in 1956. Commenced: 11 July 1952. It was repealed by section 23 of the Identification Act, Act No 72 of 1986.

100. **Gerrymandering** - is the process of designing electoral districts (the geographical area for which a representative is elected) to favor a particular party. Gerrymandering is a form of redistribution in which electoral district or constituency boundaries are deliberately modified for electoral advantage. Gerrymandering may be used to help or hinder particular constituents, such as members of a political, racial, linguistic, religious or class group. "The term gerrymandering is derived from Elbridge Gerry (1744–1814), the governor of Massachusetts from 1810 to 1812. It is a portmanteau of Gerry and salamander; the districts drawn in this case were shaped like a salamander. The term first appeared in the Boston Gazette on March 26, 1812. In 1812, Governor Gerry signed a bill into law that redistricted his state to benefit his Democratic-Republican party. He is known best for being the namesake of gerrymandering."[cxii]

101. **Oregon Black Exclusion Laws** – the Territory of Oregon encompassed an area the included the current states of Oregon, Washington, and Idaho, as well as parts of Wyoming and Montano. "There are few people who are aware of Oregon's

history of blatant racism, including its refusal to ratify the 14th and 15th Amendments of the Constitution. Oregon, America's first and only state to begin as "whites-only". When Oregon entered the Union in 1859 — it did so as a "whites-only" state. The original state constitution banned slavery, but also excluded nonwhites from living there.

Oregon Country's provisional government, which was led by Peter Burnett, a former slaver holder who came west from Missouri by wagon train, passed the law in 1844 — 15 years before Oregon became a state. The law allowed slave holders to keep their slaves for a maximum of three years. After the grace period, all black people — those considered freed or enslaved — were required to leave Oregon Country. Black women were given three years to get out; black men were required to leave in two.

The law became known as the "Peter Burnett Lash Law." Burnett, who also opposed Chinese migration to Oregon Country, would later become the first American governor of California. The "Lash Law" was quickly amended and then repealed. No black people were ever lashed under the law.

The Oregon constitution excluded blacks. In 1857, as Oregon sought to become a state, it wrote the exclusion of blacks into its constitution: "No free negro or mulatto, not residing in this State at the time of the adoption of this constitution, shall ever come, reside, or be within this State, or hold any real estate, or make any contract, or maintain any suit therein; and the Legislative Assembly shall provide by penal laws for the removal by public officers of all such free negroes and mulattoes, and for their effectual exclusion from the State, and for the punishment of persons who shall bring them into the State, or employ or harbor them therein."

Oregon has a defiant history of resisting federal laws that gave black people rights. Oregon was one of just six states that refused to ratify the 15th Amendment, which gave black men the right to vote. Oregon did not ratify the 15th amendment until 1959 — one hundred years after the state joined the Union. It was a symbolic adoption as part of its centennial celebration. It did not re-ratify the 14th amendment until 1973."[cxiii]

102. **World Wars I and II** - there was a significant amount of racism during World War I and II, as Black soldiers were in segregated units separate from White soldiers but under the command of White officers; some of whom were the children of Confederate Soldiers. During both wars, African Americans were segregated from the whites and had their own squadron. They are not allowed to be conjoin with white squads. They were relegated to being cooks and orderlies in the Navy. They were grave markers and diggers in the Army and also relegated to cooks and orderlies. They basically were not allowed to fight. That is why the Tuskegee Airmen are so important in our History. They fought for the right to fight for the country. They were highly sought after by the commanders. They never lost a bomber they were escorting. When the war was over with, they returned home to the very racist society. Things slowly started to change for them in society which led to the start of the Civil Rights movement.

103. **Wars on Indigenous People Throughout the World** – have been the subject and genocide by dominant cultures throughout human history. Their cultures are different from other cultures who took advantage of them and the territories they occupied which contained raw materials and resources they wanted. In every case, the oppressors fundamentally forced their will on the indigenous population by any means necessary including war driving them off their own land and placing them in reservations. The dominant culture viewed their takeover as natural in the social evolution of humans as part of the survival of the fittest concept.

104. **Vietnam War** - the reasons behind American opposition to the Vietnam War fell into the following main categories:

opposition to the draft; moral, legal, and pragmatic arguments against U.S. intervention and reaction to the media portrayal of the devastation in Southeast Asia.

The Draft, as a system of conscription which threatened lower class registrants and middle-class registrants alike, drove much of the protest after 1965. Conscientious objectors did play an active role although their numbers were small. The prevailing sentiment that the draft was unfairly administered inflamed blue-collar American and African-American opposition to the military draft itself.

Opposition to the war arose during a time of unprecedented student activism which followed the free speech movement and the civil rights movement. The military draft mobilized the baby boomers who were most at risk but grew to include a varied cross-section of Americans. The growing opposition to the Vietnam War was partly attributed to greater access to uncensored information presented by the extensive television coverage on the ground in Vietnam.

105. **Pearl Harbor** - The Japanese attacked Pearl Harbor for a number of reasons. The main reason being President Roosevelt banning all exports of scrap iron, steel and oil to Japan. Japan had lost more than 90% of its oil supply. Other causes which sparked the attack included the belief that Japan was becoming encircled by Western powers which would affect its nationality pride. Other causes include the fear of resources such as oil running low. Japan had a strong determination of advancing in the East Asia region. The United States demanded the Japanese withdrawal from Indo-China and opposed its expansion efforts. Japan felt that its demands were not being achieved by diplomacy. The Japanese were keen on expanding their empire and had to decide between surrendering or going to war with the United States

There has also been knowledge that racial superiority made the Americans underestimate the Japanese and how a war game simulation of such an attack had been run and then ignored.

106. **Public Education** - like most institutions, racial inequality in education is still present in today's society. Many students from disadvantage backgrounds have potential but did not have the opportunity to strengthen their skills due to the inequality in the education system. Programs need to be developed to eliminate inequality and provide subordinate group members with the tools they need to do well in school. Minority students are expelled and suspended at three times the rate of white students. They are not offered the variety of courses that white students are, and they are taught by teachers with less experience. These factors can hinder a student's chance at success in higher education and in a career. Steps that will be taken in the future to end education inequality. With some changes, all students can have equal opportunities for success in their lives. The key is resolving the massive disparities in school quality and discipline that federal data tells us begin in pre-kindergarten classrooms.

Schools around the United States and particular the South, were segregated. By the 1970's, due to federal court orders, most became integrated. Since 2000, federal judges have released hundreds of school districts from court forced integration and many have returned toward segregation. Subordinate group children now attend more segregated schools today and their achievement gap between other racial groups which had narrowed since the 1970's is now widening in many jurisdictions.

107. **Public (including Mental Health abuse and homicidal conduct)** – there are two prevailing thoughts on racism and mental health. Some believe racism is taught and a learned behavior that happens out of fear and ignorance. Others believe racism is a mental disorder. For some people, racism is so deeply ingrained in them that there appear to be a type of mental

disorder. There are also numerous examples that racism can be unlearned. Once someone sees that a person who is different than them isn't a threat to them or their beliefs, the person can change how they think and feel about other racial groups. Mental health assistance has been minimized in many societies, including the United States. Mental health care suffered drastic cuts were made in the 1980's at the federal and state levels that have not been recovered.

The Transatlantic Slave Trade and its aftermath created mental health issues with some subordinate group members in which few ever received mental health assistance after generations of racism, prejudices, biases and disparate treatment. Furthermore, some dominant culture members who had racism ingrained in them at an early age, could also benefit from some type of mental health assistance. Mental health eludes many in our world, thus resulting in considerable distress, stigma, and isolation.

108. **Genocide of Australian Aborigines that killed 90% of their populations in less than a century -** The European invasion in 1788 resulted in the Indigenous population dropping from circa 1 million to about 0.1 million in the first 100 years as a result of introduced disease, dispossession from traditional lands, economy and food resources, and massacres by gangs of well-armed, horse-mounted Europeans. The remaining Indigenous populations were variously subject to racist "protection" Acts and confinement to reserves with an ethnocide policy of removal of hundreds of thousands of Indigenous children from their mothers. The National Inquiry into the separation of the children concluded that between one-in-three and one-in-ten Indigenous children were forcibly removed from their families and communities in the period from approximately 1910 until 1970.

109. **9/11 -** the major world event of 9/11 saw an increase of Arab Americans that were profiled, feared, detained, assaulted, accused, interrogated, harassed, hated, and collectivized. The event of 9/11 brought the country together over a shared enemy and as a result many Arabs were scrutinized in their daily activities in the United States and around the world. The event of 9/11 was a cowardly unprovoked attack was against civilians with no military objective. Throughout the history of America, many racial groups have experience racial, religious and other prejudice in this nation, particularly African Americans and the indigenous people but 9/11 highlighted the Arab people from this major single event. Islamist extremists were responsible for this atrocity but due to national security issues, racial group members were targeted similar to Japanese Americans during WWII. The event of 9/11 was an attack on all Americans and their racial groups, so people of all groups came together for a short time. We even forgave our differences and focused on the event that united us as a country. Unfortunately, it takes an event of this magnitude to unite all racial groups and it was short lived.

110. **Rwanda** - the Genocide was the 1994 mass killing of hundreds of thousands of Rwanda's Tutsi and Hutu political moderates by Hutu under the Hutu Power ideology. Over the course of approximately 100 days, from the assassination of Juvénal Habyarimana on 6 April through mid-July, at least 500,000 people were killed. Most estimates indicate a death toll between 800,000 and 1,000,000, which could be as high as 20% of the total population.

The genocide had its roots in the Hutu-Tutsi ethnic divide and related sporadic violence, which had resulted in a large number of Tutsi refugees in the nations around Rwanda by 1990. In that year, the Rwandan Patriotic Front (RPF), a rebel group composed mostly of Tutsi refugees, invaded. The Rwandan Civil War fought between the Hutu regime, with support from Francophone.

111. **Bosnia** - Bosnia tried to break away from Yugoslavia in 1992 and eventually succeeded. Yugoslavia tried to suppress Bosnian secession and during the war events of genocide did occur. There are 3 main ethnic groups in Bosnia. There are Bosnian Serbs (Orthodox Christian), Bosnian Croats (Roman Catholic) and Bosniaks who are Muslim. In 1992 Bosnia had a referendum on independence from Yugoslavia, the Bosniaks and Bosnian Croats wanted independence the Bosnian Serbs did not. They wanted a union with Serbia (the country). The Yugoslav army (JNA) armed the Bosnian Serbs and they began to attack all of Bosnia that was not Serbian.

The genocide or ethnic cleansing involved expelling and/or killing non-Serbs from towns and cities, their victims were mostly Bosniaks (Muslims) but also Bosnian Croats. Later, the Bosnian Croats (who initially helped the Bosniaks) committed their own genocides against the Bosniaks and the Bosniaks did the same to the Croats. The Bosniaks and Croats made a truce in 1994. The largest single massacre took place at Srebrenica in 1995, when Bosnian Serbs killed 8,000 Bosniak men and boys. Overall, over

100,000 Bosnian (Croat, Muslim and Serb) were killed and two million missing or displaced.

112. **Darfur**- the Genocide began in February 2003, when rebellions were started by the Justice and Equality Movement (JEM) and the Sudanese Liberation Army (SLA), who accused the government of oppressing non-Arabs and favoring the Arabs and neglecting the Darfur region in West Sudan. The Sudanese government responded with aerial bombardments, join-strikes on tribes with the Janjaweed. Together with the Sudanese Military they have consistently burnt down villages and displaced over 2,500,000 people. Together they have killed between 200,000 to 400,000 people. The government has restricted the press and put many people in jail to silence the opposition.

113. **Chinese Head Tax in Canada** – The Chinese head tax was levied on Chinese immigration to Canada between 1885 and 1993, under the Chinese Immigration Act (1885). With few exceptions, Chinese people had to pay $50 (later raised to $100, and then $500) to come to Canada. This anti-Chinese legislation was the first in Canadian history to exclude immigration on the basis of ethnic origin. When the tax was removed from the Chinese Immigration Act in 1923, Chinese immigration was banned until 1947[cxiv]

114. **Aboriginal Children Removed from their Families** – A decade ago, the Prime Minister of Australia issued a national apology to the Aborigines for the racism they endured since the British invasion. But day-to-day life haven't improved much for many Aborigines – particularly children. The number of indigenous children taken out of their homes and placed in care has increased more than 60 percent.[cxv] While race-based legislation may be gone, Aboriginal children are being removed from their families at a higher rate than ever before. While the majority of Australians condemn overt racism, Aboriginal children are quietly being taken away from parents under policy

that allows racism to thrive at an institutional level. Raising awareness about the Stolen Generation has mostly worked, but this education has not led to the structural change needed to stop Aboriginal children from being taken from their families.[cxvi]

115. **Chinese Head Tax in New Zealand** - New Zealand imposed a poll tax on Chinese immigrants during the 19th and early 20th centuries. The poll tax was effectively lifted in the 1930s following the invasion of China by Japan and was finally repealed in 1944. Prime Minister at the time Helen Clark offered New Zealand's Chinese community an official apology for the poll tax on 12 February 2002. Although Chinese immigrants were invited to New Zealand by the Dunedin Chamber of Commerce, prejudice against them quickly led to calls for restrictions on immigration.

Following the example of anti-Chinese poll taxes enacted by California in 1852 and by Australian states in the 1850s, 1860s and 1870s, John Hall's government passed the Chinese Immigration Act 1881. This imposed a 10 tax per Chinese person entering New Zealand and permitted only one Chinese immigrant for every 10 tons of cargo. Richard Seddon's government increased the tax to 100 per head in 1896 and tightened the other restriction to only one Chinese immigrant for every 200 tons of cargo.

An estimated 4500 people paid the poll tax, raising over 300,000 (worth about 28 million in 2001).[cxvii]

PART FIVE - GLOBAL RACIAL TRANSFORMATION AND THE RESETTING OF GLOBAL RACIAL CHANGE

In the context of the existing world racial order, long-held beliefs of the dominant culture's superiority over the other racial groups as well as being the rulers of the world economically, culturally, socially and politically are being challenged and contested. However, racial dominance around the globe is very complicated, and urgently needs to be understood and dislodged. The conquering of most of the world by the Europeans during the fifteenth through nineteenth centuries by the dominant group's ancestors only managed to blur racial lines and distinctions in many parts of the world, global land borders and integrate racial groups across the line. In many instances, it resulted in a devasting adverse consequences on those territories and the world for many members of the subordinate groups. The Europeans, however, achieved their stated goals and objectives that they set out to do in the fifteenth century.

In the coming decades, we can expect an unprecedented resetting of global racial historiography in the world covering all the established systems and institutions. There is expected to be an increased heightened political rhetoric, activity and awareness that will continue to question the fundamental values and institutions in the world. The subordinate racial groups will receive pushback from the dominant culture in their quest to receive some semblance of parity and equality. The subordinate racial groups must liberate themselves from the current domination of the dominant racial group. The strategies for achieving true human equalities will be discussed in the final part.

The full acknowledgment of global racism is the first step towards dismantling it. "The failure to acknowledge race as a

143

fundamental feature of today's unequal world order remains a striking weakness of radical as well as conventional analyses of that order. Current global and national socioeconomic hierarchies are not mere residues of a bygone era of primitive accumulation. Just as it should be inconceivable to address the past, present, and future of American society without giving central attention to the role of African American struggles, so analyzing and addressing twenty first century structures of global inequality requires giving central attention to Africa."[cxviii] "The many events by the European countries in the fifteenth century contributed heavily to the unequal values given to human lives in the world racial order, both between and within countries and continents. These inequalities are shaped by multiple factors including race. But they are also molded by a long history that systematically makes the African continent, those who live there, and those who come from there particularly vulnerable."[cxix]

Several past and present global inequalities since the European's domination of the world in the fifteenth century are listed in part four. There have been numerous world events that occurred during the past one and one-half century that transformed the world's view on race relations, but this part will deal with three major pivotal events which helped shaped and defined the racial issues that we are experiencing today. The slavery in the Americas, the South Africa Apartheid and the Holocaust were watershed events in recent world human history.

The unpeaceful end of slavery in the United States with the Civil War in the 1860s and the Holocaust during World War II, and the peaceful end of Apartheid in South Africa in the early 1990s stand among the greatest human achievements in the nineteenth and twentieth centuries. These events transformed the world by socially displaying the ultimate forms of global racism. These were the most important events in shaping the world as we know it now. From a global perspective, it is near impossible to overstate their centrality to almost every feature of life pertaining to changing the dynamics of race relations world-wide as we presently know it. A discussion about the Holocaust, the South Africa Apartheid and Slavery in the Americas is particularly important, but they are not isolated events.

The twenty and twenty-first centuries also saw numerous other acts of horrific violence ranging from Ze-Dong Mao (China, 1958-61 and 1966-69, Tibet 1949-50), Leopold II of Belgium (Congo, 1886-1908), Jozef Stalin (USSR, 1932-39), Hideki Tojo (Japan, 1941-44), Ismail Enver (Ottoman Turkey, 1915-20), Pol Pot (Cambodia, 1975-79), Yakubu Gowon (Biafra, 1967-1970), Leonid Brezhnev (Afghanistan, 1979-1982), Jean Kambanda (Rwanda, 1994) to Mullah Omar - Taliban (Afghanistan, 1986-2001).[cxx] These events and their aftermaths also had a profound effect on societies in the Americas, Europe, Asia, Africa, the Middle East and other parts of the world.

The aftermath of slavery in the United States involving the Reconstruction period, the post Reconstruction period, the Great Migration, World War II, the Civil Rights movement and the post-Civil Rights movement period will be examined in this part. In addition, this part will examine the South African Apartheid, the Holocaust and Brazil, Europe and the United States' current racial issues.

Slavery in the United States and its aftermath is examined because it propelled the nation to the status of the world's sole superpower that exists today although fewer slaves from the Transatlantic Slave Trade went to its territory. Although the United States received far fewer African slaves than other countries in the Americas, its past and current impact of the globe is much more prominent. "The United States relies more on market mechanisms than any other highly industrialized nation in the world."[cxxi] It has been more than 150 years since the end of the Civil War to end the enslavement of African Americans and more than 60 years after the Civil Rights movement to end the legal subjugation of them. The struggles over slavery gave the United States a Civil War, a Reconstruction period, segregation, Jim Crow laws and Black Codes, and finally a Civil Rights movement.

The seeds were sown for the Civil Rights movement for Africa Americans in America after the Civil War when the slaves were freed. This momentum continued during World War II. It also continued until legalized segregation and Jim Crow laws were abolished in the 1960s. It also is still prevalent in a more sophisticated form in the twenty-first century.

Decades after Apartheid in South Africa and after legal racial segregation officially ended in the United States, both countries are still immersed in race tension. Just changing the laws or taking them off the book in no way erases the after effects of centuries of economic, cultural, social and political structural inequality that are largely racial.

The South African Apartheid and the United States Civil Rights movement struggles changed and transformed the world racial social order although Apartheid did not end until the 1990's, some thirty years after the civil right movement in America. These struggles may have affected other countries around the world and opened the way for other subordinate groups whose rights were being trampled on by the dominant culture to seek justice and recognition in the country of their residing. "If the most oppressed subordinate group make their countries and the world stop and listen to its grievances and act to redress some of them, certainly other subordinate groups could achieve no less."[cxxii]

The aftermath of the Holocaust led to the creation of the country of Israel in 1948 as a place where Jews would be safer. But the creation of the state of Israel has led to much of the unrest in the Middle East ever since that continues today. "The situation of Palestine and Israel is very contentious. While Arabs and Jews technically do not belong to different races, their religious and cultural differences and the political history of the region has contributed to extremities and tensions. Yet, this is more complex than a clash of religions and races, as deeper an issue is the geopolitical and economic activities of the past decades and centuries that have fueled these social tensions."[cxxiii] However, other unrest such as the conflicts between Sunni and Shiite Muslims also exist in the Middle East.

The slavery in Brazil is also examined because the country received by far the highest percentage of African slaves during the Transatlantic Slave Trade. Although Brazil's present global impact was not as prominent as the United States, the aftermath of slavery in Brazil differs somewhat from the United States in certain respects. I will examine how the two countries dealt with the legacy of slavery in their societies from a political, social, cultural and economic perspective.

The United States and the continent of Europe face common political problems. The two political entities have a common bond, shared goals and overlapping interests. They have formed a Transatlantic partnership that have existed since the beginning of the Transatlantic Trade Slave in the fifteenth century. Furthermore, most of United States' citizens have European ancestry.

All these issues and events have transformed, challenged and reset the changes of the world racial order after the Transatlantic Slave Trade ended in the nineteen centuries. The impacts of racism that subordinate groups experience from these events are far-reaching and have long lasting consequences. These events have left an indelible cultural legacy which will still take decades or even centuries to repair.

RECONSTRUCTION

In the United States, African Americans were granted the freedom from slavery via the Emancipation Proclamation signed by President Abraham Lincoln in 1863. The Emancipation Proclamation freed the slaves on the terms of the oppressors and hence was not a true liberation by any means. The United States Civil War was followed by decades of racial discrimination in every part of the country.

Reconstruction was the period in American history (1865-1877) immediately after the United States Civil War. The physical rebuilding of southern cities, ports, railroads, and farms that had been destroyed during the war was a small part of Reconstruction.

The Civil War ended on April 9, 1865, when Confederate general Robert E. Lee surrendered to Union general Ulysses S. Grant at Appomattox Courthouse in Virginia. The North's victory settled two important issues. First, it established that states were not allowed to leave, or secede from, the United States. Second, it put an end to slavery throughout the country. But the end of the war also raised a whole new set of issues. For example, federal lawmakers had to decide whether to punish the Confederate leaders, what process to use to readmit the Southern states to the Union, and how much assistance was needed to provide in securing equal rights for the freed slaves?

Because these complicated issues carried a great deal of importance for the future of the nation. Reconstruction was a time of great political and social turmoil. President Andrew Johnson who took office after Abraham Lincoln was assassinated in 1865 controlled the earliest Reconstruction efforts. But the U.S. Congress felt that the president's Reconstruction policies were too lenient on the South. Led by members of the Republican Party, Congress enacted stricter Reconstruction policies beginning in

1866 and sent in federal troops to enforce them. The ongoing dispute between Johnson and Congress led to the president's impeachment (a trial to decide whether to remove him from office) in 1868.[cxxiv]

In the United States, life after slavery was a new world for African Americans. They were very resilient people. Most were set free after slavery haphazardly with little resources from the government or their owners to deal with their new realities. Four million African slaves were finally set free with no education, money, land, housing, little food, towns, and hope for employment. They were trying to figure out how to survive. Yet, they wanted to be treated as human beings and some decided to stay on the former owner's plantation to work as share croppers. Others celebrated their newborn freedoms by explored new areas of the country for better living conditions and a new way of life. They never received their 'forty acres and a mule' which they were promise. For a moment, they were free from the indignity of being enslaved, sexual assaults, and the denial of education and homeownership. Most notably with this freedom they were free to run for office.

Africa Americans practiced the rights, opportunities, and responsibilities that came with legal citizenship. Seven hundred African Americans even served in elected public office, including two United States Senators and fourteen members of the United States House of Representatives between 1865 and 1877. Another 1,300 Black men and women held appointed government jobs.[cxxv]

It was very common to find thriving all-Black towns across the country in places where Black people filled all seats in public office and worked in favor of Black interest from the local to federal level.

There were even Black elected officials in areas with substantial white populations. For a while, both conservative and liberal whites partnered with Blacks for political purposes, pitting whites against each other.

Under Congressional Reconstruction, the Southern states adopted new constitutions and formed governments that allowed the participation of black people. These states were then permitted to rejoin the Union. But it did not take long for the process to begin to fall apart. But from the sidelines, some European Americans disgruntled lurked. They carefully watched Black people progress from slavery's torment towards self-sufficiency and independence. Many Southern whites continued to believe that blacks were inferior to them and should not have equal rights. Violence erupted throughout the South as whites rebelled against Congress's Reconstruction policies. Blacks were intimidated and terrorized so that they would not vote, and political leadership in the South gradually returned to the hands of whites. This era of black excellence came to an end as groups such the KKK violently enacted their hatred against Black people.

Reconstruction officially ended in 1877, when President Rutherford B. Hayes withdrew federal troops from the South. The withdrawal of federal troops from the South afforded hateful whites to ban laws that supported Black people's progress, replacing them with Black Codes that allowed lynching and disenfranchisement to reign supreme again. Jim Crow segregation began in areas where it did not exist before. This was another opportunity to reassert their authority.

But even though Reconstruction failed to ensure equality for black citizens in the United States, it set the stage and paved the way for the Civil Rights Movement (1950's and 1960's) that would take place nearly a century later. It took nearly a century after the civil rights movement under the leadership of Dr. Martin Luther King for Black society to begin climbing back up the political ladder.

These events still affect many of their descendants to this very day. In the United States, it involved two hundred and fifty years of slavery and forced servitude, ninety years of Jim Crow laws with separate and unequal laws and the current ongoing struggles.

THE PERIOD AFTER RECONSTUCTION – JIM CROW LAWS & BLACK CODES

After the Civil War ended and Reconstruction period began, the Republican party established certain laws that forbade white Southerners from mistreating African Americans. Then after the Reconstruction era ended, Southern lawmakers came up with the Jim Crow laws. They were laws to prohibit certain freedoms from African Americans. Segregation was one of the major components of this law.

Jim Crow was the system in the Southern United States from the 1880s to 1964 in which African Americans were segregated in public schools and public places and had little or no political power or civil rights. It was a low point in Black history after the euphoria of Reconstruction. The Jim Crow laws were state and local laws enacted primarily but not exclusively in the Southern and border states of the United States between 1876 and 1965. They mandated segregation in all public facilities, with a "separate but equal" status for black Americans and members of other non-white racial groups.

The origin of the phrase "Jim Crow" has often been attributed to "Jump Jim Crow", a song-and-dance caricature of African Americans performed by white actor Thomas D. Rice in blackface, which first surfaced in 1832 and was used to satirize Andrew Jackson's populist policies.

Jim Crow laws were created in the American South after the Civil War. They manipulated the spirit of the Emancipation

Proclamation and the letter of the federal law to ensure that White dominance of African Americans would continue even after it was illegal to own slaves.

Jim Crow laws were declared illegal by the US Supreme Court when they voted against the school system in Brown v. Board of Education, and later laws such the Civil Rights Act and Voting Rights Act.

Although there really weren't Jim Crow laws in Northern or Western states like there was in the South, institutional racism existed outside the South and does so today.

The Jim Crow laws were separate from the 1800 - 1866 Black Codes, which had also restricted the civil rights and civil liberties of African Americans. State-sponsored school segregation was declared unconstitutional by the Supreme Court of the United States in 1954 in Brown v. Board of Education. Generally, the remaining Jim Crow laws were overruled by the Civil Rights Act of 1964 and the Voting Rights Act of 1965.[cxxvi]

Examples of mistreatment:

- Separate entry doors and seating in movie theatres.
- Poll Taxes and literacy tests to qualify to vote.
- Seating in the back of the bus or separate train cars and waiting rooms.
- Separate dining facilities.
- Separate bathroom facilities.
- Separate water fountains.
- Separate churches.
- Separate hotels and bank tellers.
- Separate public and State parks.
- Separate schools and books could not be interchanged.
- Separate doctors, hospitals, graveyards and undertakers.
- Curfews.

- A ban on mixed-race dating and marriage, and mixed marriages declared illegal.
- Separate public phone booths, ball parks and ball park seating.
- Separate areas in public libraries.
- Separate jails and prisons.

The Black Codes were laws passed on the state and local level in the United States to restrict the civil rights and civil liberties of Black Americans, particularly former slaves in former Confederate states.

In 1865 and 1866, state governments in the South enacted laws designed to regulate the lives of the former slaves. These measures, differing from state to state, were revisions of the earlier slave codes that had regulated that institution.[cxxvii]

Although the Black Codes are most commonly associated with the Southern states after the American Civil War and the Reconstruction, where they were used to regulate the freedoms of former slaves, Black Codes developed over the span of half a century or more and some laws date to the early nineteenth century in Northern states. Black Codes was a name given to laws passed by southern governments established during the presidency of Andrew Johnson. These laws imposed severe restrictions on freed slaves such as prohibiting their right to vote, forbidding them to sit on juries, limiting their right to testify against white men, carrying weapons in public places and working in certain occupations

The Black Codes of 1865 turned out to be a unique way for white southerners to attempt to maintain the way of life they had known prior to the Civil War. While freedom had been won, ex-slaves were restricted, and opportunities were limited.[cxxviii] They were early segregationist attempts in the new world to keep blacks from gaining power, wealth, or mixing with whites. They predate the civil war and additional black codes were enacted after the Civil War.

THE GREAT MIGRATION

Humankind has practiced migration and vagility since the beginning of history all over the world. This is an ongoing phenomenon which is always occurring somewhere around the world. People migrate for several reasons including looking for a better way of life, escape widespread brutal racism, poverty, famine and atrocities, religious persecution, economic and job opportunities and educational opportunities, etc. The migration of Europeans from Europe to North American, South America, Africa, Asia, Australia, New Zealand, the Caribbean and other parts of the world during the fifteenth to the twentieth century during the Transatlantic Slave Trade was arguably the largest migration in world history.

This part will discuss the Great Migration in the United States that involved the movement of approximately six million Black people out of the Southern United States to the North, Midwest and Western states from 1916 to 1970. This pattern of shifting population accelerated because of World War I and continued throughout the 1920s. The Great Migration also initiated the change from a primarily rural to a predominantly urban lifestyle for African Americans. Blacks migrated to escape widespread racism in the South, to seek employment opportunities in industrial cities of the North, to get better education for their children, and to pursue what was widely perceived to be a more prosperous life.

This was another transformational event in America that changed the landscape of the country and opened opportunities and new realities to the slaves and descendants of the slaves in their quest to harvest the freedom that they worked so hard to achieve.

There are several factors that contributed to this major movement of people within the United States:

1. A Boll Weevil infestation of the cotton fields of the South in the late 1910s, forced many sharecroppers to search for employment opportunities elsewhere;
2. This was exacerbated by a drop-in cotton prices, which meant that landowners could no longer afford to hire outside workers and tenant farmers could no longer afford to pay their rents;
3. World War I and strict legislation limited immigration into the United States effectively put a halt to the flow of European immigrants to the emerging industrial and manufacturing centers Northeast and Midwest, causing shortages of workers in the factories.
4. Anti-immigration legislation after the war similarly resulted in a dire shortage of workers;
5. The Great Mississippi Flood of 1927 and its aftermath displaced hundreds of thousands of African-American farm workers;
6. While they still existed in the North, racial prejudices were less likely to result in severe violence and terror campaigns against the African American population, such as that waged by the newly reemerged Ku Klux Klan;
7. The Great Depression caused people to seek new employment opportunities;
8. Even before America's entry into World War II, industrial production in the Northeast and Midwest increased rapidly because of Cash and Carry and the Lend-Lease Act, and people were needed to staff the factories.

The scope of the mass migration is best seen in Detroit, Michigan, a city which, during World War II, earned the title of "Arsenal of Democracy" for its contribution to the war effort. In 1910, the African American population of Detroit was just 6,000, but this jumped to 120,000 by the time of the Stock Market Crash of 1929. Other cities, such as Chicago and New York City also experienced enormous surges in their African American population.

The Great Migration provided unprecedented economic and educational opportunities for African Americans. Adults were earning higher wages while their children were presented with better educational opportunities. Furthermore, because of war needs and the rising population of African Americans in the industrial centers, in 1943 President Roosevelt's Executive Order 8002, banning racial discrimination in the workplace in all industries involved in the war effort and paving the way for the civil rights movement.

Their migration eventually changed the landscape of the North and the South. Now there seems to be a reverse migration back to the South. In the last two decades of the twentieth century, a new movement of African Americans within the United States began and has reached enough magnitude to be termed by some as a second Great Migration. Since roughly 1980, large numbers of African Americans have been moving from other parts of the country to the South. These migrants are typically the descendants of those who had left the South in the original Great Migration.

As in the first Great Migration, this movement has been motivated by economic opportunities, this time in booming Southern cities. The primary magnet for the new migrants has been Atlanta, although almost all Southern cities have seen a large influx of native-born African Americans. This movement has been heavily driven by the best-educated African Americans.[cxxix]

At the beginning of the Great Migration, African Americans had to migrate because of the conditions listed above. However, the political, social and economic implications would be a lot differently in the South today if most blacks had stayed put. It would not be presumptive that Blacks would have been the majority populations in several Southern states. There would also have been a very good possibility that blacks could be controlling some governorships, state house legislators & local politics in some of the Southern states with large African American populations. Now their influence is dispersed around the country, but the demographics are changing every decade.

WORLD WAR II

The experience of black American soldier during the Second World War was the main cause of increase pressure for civil rights after 1945. Military service was rigidly segregated by race and defined the nonwhite soldier as inferior in every way. World War II also proved to be the cauldron from which dramatic changes in race relations would come forth. An argument can be made that the beginning of the modern civil rights movement can be traced to the national wartime experience, and these domestic events, as well as the imperative of dealing with a different world would influence changes in how United States foreign policy would deal with racial issues in international affairs.

Racism continued as a sometime expressed element in American foreign policy through the 1920s and 1930s. World War II, however, set in motion events that resulted in a change in attitude on race both domestically and in foreign policy. Ambivalence on racial issues marked the U.S. record during the war. On the one hand, the tradition of white supremacy and racial prejudice, enforced through segregation, in many ways remained the standard of race relations in American society.

Military service was rigidly segregated by race and defined the nonwhite soldier as inferior in every way. It was disheartening to see decorated war heroes who fought valiantly for their country but only return to a society to be refused accommodation, work and the right to eat in diners and still must live with segregation. Their contribution to the war effort helped to generate a desire for change and a belief that they should fight for equality.

The world racial order that emerged from the war was one in which a handful of western European nations no longer were supreme over most of the world's populations.

Although this new emphasis was pragmatic in nature, it also was shaped by undeniable changes in attitude toward race that were occurring in other global societies. By the end of the 1960s, the colonies once held by European nations had largely disappeared. Nonwhite populations were assuming control of their own fate around the world, and proponents of white supremacy were increasingly on the defensive. During the war the United States had condemned the racism inherent in Nazi German society. Postwar policies increasingly reflected a condemnation of racial prejudice.[cxxx]

World War II marked the end of European Colonialism in Europe. The war bankrupted and destroyed the former great European powers. The United Kingdom ended up relinquishing many of its Colonies. In Africa, every single Colony eventually became independent. Ethiopia, which had been independent until the invasion by Italy, regained its independence.

THE UNITED STATES CIVIL RIGHTS MOVEMENT

The Civil Rights Movement (1954–1968) refers to the reform movements in the United States aimed at outlawing racial discrimination against African Americans particularly in the South. During the period, acts of civil disobedience produced crisis situations between protesters and government authorities. The authorities of federal, state, and local governments often had to respond immediately to crisis situations which highlighted the inequalities faced by African Americans. There were forms of civil disobedience involving organized boycotts, student protests and mass marches.

MAJOR TIMELINES IN THE CIVIL RIGHTS MOVEMENT

May 17, 1954

The Supreme Court ruled on the landmark case Brown v. Board of Education of Topeka, Kansas unanimously agreeing that segregation in public schools is unconstitutional. The ruling paved the way for large-scale desegregation. The decision overturned the 1896 Plessy v. Ferguson ruling that sanctioned "separate but equal" segregation of the races, ruling that "separate educational facilities are inherently unequal." It was a victory for National Advancement Association for Colored People (NAACP) and their attorney Thurgood Marshall, who was later appointed to the Supreme Court as the nation's first black justice.

August 1955

Fourteen-year-old Chicagoan Emmett Till was visiting family in Mississippi when he is kidnapped, brutally beaten, shot, and dumped in the Tallahatchie River for allegedly whistling at a white woman. Two white men, J. W. Milam and Roy Bryant, are arrested for the murder and acquitted by an all-white jury. They later boast about committing the murder in a Look magazine interview. The case became a major catalyst of the civil rights movement.

December 1, 1955

In Montgomery, Alabama, NAACP member Rosa Parks refused to give up her seat at the front of the "colored section" of a bus to a white passenger, defying a southern custom of the time. In response to her arrest the Montgomery black community launched a bus boycott, which will last for more than a year, until the buses are desegregated Dec. 21, 1956. As newly elected president of the Montgomery Improvement Association (MIA), Reverend Martin Luther King, Jr., was instrumental in leading the boycott and later emerged as the leader of the civil rights movement.

September 1957
In Little Rock, Arkansas, formerly all-white Central High School was forced to integrate the school. Nine black students are blocked from entering the school on the orders of Governor Orval Faubus. President Eisenhower sends federal troops and the National Guard to intervene on behalf of the students, who become known as the "Little Rock Nine."

May 4, 1961

Over the spring and summer, student volunteers begin taking bus trips through the South to test out new laws that prohibit segregation in interstate travel facilities, which included bus and railway stations. Several of the groups of "freedom riders," as they are called, were attacked by angry mobs along the way. The program sponsored by The Congress of Racial Equality (CORE) and the Student Nonviolent Coordinating Committee (SNCC), involves more than 1,000 volunteers, black and white.

October 1, 1962

James Meredith becomes the first black student to enroll at the University of Mississippi in Oxford, Mississippi. Violence and riots surrounding the incident cause President Kennedy to send 5,000 federal troops.

April 16, 1963

Martin Luther King is arrested and jailed during anti-segregation protests in Birmingham, Alabama. He wrote his seminal "Letter from Birmingham Jail," arguing that individuals have the moral duty to disobey unjust laws.

May,1963

During civil rights protests in Birmingham, Ala., Commissioner of Public Safety Eugene "Bull" Connor uses fire hoses and police dogs on black demonstrators. These images of brutality, which were televised and published widely were instrumental in gaining sympathy for the civil rights movement around the world.

June 12, 1963

In Jackson, Mississippi, Mississippi's NAACP field secretary, 37-year-old Medgar Evers, was murdered outside his home. Byron De La Beckwith is tried twice in 1964, both trials resulting in hung juries. Thirty years later he was convicted for murdering Evers.

August 28, 1963

In Washington, D.C., about 200,000 people join the March on Washington congregating at the Lincoln Memorial. Participants listen as Martin Luther King delivers his famous "I Have a Dream" speech.

1964 and 1965

The Civil Rights Act of 1964 was followed by the Voting Rights Act in 1965, laws which helped change the lives of black Americans. The first major law was the Civil Rights Act of 1964 which banned racial discrimination in employment and gave black Americans equal rights to enter all public places and bodies. This aimed to end discrimination in schools, hospitals, cinemas, restaurants and on public transport. The Voting Rights Act of 1965 took away the obstacles which had prevented non-whites from voting and banned such things as the use of literacy tests to qualify for voting rights. The Fair Housing Act of 1968 made it illegal to discriminate in the housing market. Through these laws Americans of all races were granted civil rights and legal protection of those rights.

1966

By 1966, the emergence of the Black Power Movement, which lasted roughly from 1966 to 1975, enlarged the aims of the Civil Rights Movement to include racial dignity, economic and political self-sufficiency, and freedom from oppression by whites. While King's approach took on peaceful protests, some blacks under the influence of Malcolm X, Louis Farrakhan, Stokely Carmichael and the Black Panthers party adopted more forceful forms of protest.

They helped formed the Black Power movement and they were prepared to use other means to push for change. The late 1960s and 1970s saw riots in many US cities as young black males, frustrated at being unemployed or having low-paid jobs and living in ghetto environments, took to the streets in protest.

The National Association for the Advancement of Colored People (NAACP) was founded in 1909 and it struggled to end race discrimination through litigation, education, and lobbying efforts. Its crowning achievement was its legal victory in the Supreme Court decision Brown v. Board of Education (1954) that rejected separate white and colored school systems and by implication overturned the "separate but equal" doctrine established in Plessy v. Ferguson.

The National Advancement Association of Colored People (NAACP) also played a key role in the early civil rights movement in the United States. The group commissioned Gunnar Myrdal's report on black life, an American dilemma. It urged President Truman to desegregate the US military. It organized the Montgomery bus boycott. It created a system of black colleges and universities. It worked for decades to lay the legal groundwork for desegregation.

The National Association for the Advancement of Colored People realized that legislative action, either in the American South or in the U.S. Congress would be impossible in the existing setting. The powerful Southern coalition in the Congress made passage of meaningful civil rights legislation impossible. This left the courts as the one forum in which to challenge segregation. Accepting "separate but equal" as the existing rule of law, the NAACP managed a calculated effort throughout the nation to attack the notion that segregated schools were equal. From the 1920 through 1954, the NAACP continually carefully picked cases that would advance its cause. In 1954, with the Supreme Court's ruling in Brown v. Board of Education, the NAACP won the landmark victory that enabled it to attack separate as unequal. It remains one of the most important organizations fighting for equality for all people. Thurgood Marshall, an American lawyer, successfully argued several cases, including the Brown v. Board of Education. Later, from 1967 to 1991, Marshall served as an Associate Justice of the Supreme Court of the United States become its first American-Justice.

Besides the NAACP, there were several other prominent organizations such as Student Nonviolent Coordinating Committee, (SNCC), the Congress of Racial Equality (CORE) and Southern Christian Leadership Conference (SCLC), who involved in for the struggle for fundamental issues of freedom, respect, dignity, and economic and social equality.[cxxxi]

POST CIVIL RIGHTS MOVEMENT

Despite such protests, life for many African Americans did improve during the 1970s, 1980s, 1990s and into the twenty-first century. Some significant gains were made in most of the fields of their endeavors throughout most sectors of society. African Americans have overcome many obstacles to secure prominent positions in senior government positions, arts, politics, entertainment, theater, sciences, health, media, film and music, industry, and sports management and coaches.

In politics, Shirley Chisholm became the first African American woman elected to the United States Congress who served for seven terms from 1969 to 1983. In 1972, she became the first African American candidate for a major party's nomination for the President of the United States and the first woman to run for the Democratic Party's presidential nomination.[cxxxii] In 1984 and 1988, the Rev. Jesse Jackson became the first formidable candidate to run for President of the United States. In 2004, the Rev. Al Sharpton, had an unsuccessful bid in his Presidential race. In 2009,

Barack Obama became the first President of color elected as the President of the United States and leader of the free world. Colin Powell became the first African American to become Chairman of the Joint Chiefs of Staff and the Secretary of State. Condoleezza Rice also became Secretary of State. Eric Holder and Loretta Lynch became the first two African Americans to become United States Attorney General.

In sports, Muhammad Ali became the world heavyweight boxing champion in the 1960s and during the 1980s, Carl Lewis surpassed Jesse Owens to win nine Olympic gold medals and Usain Bolts of Jamaica later eclipsed Lewis as the premier sprinter in Olympic history. Michael Jordan and Lebron James became icons and universal known in the sport of basketball. In the 1990's, Tiger Woods became a legendary golfer and popularized the sports for non-white players. Pele became a legendary soccer player. African American quarterbacks and head football coaches became a norm in the National Football League as well as other professional and collegiate sports.

In television, Bill Cosby and Oprah Winfrey had top rated television shows and became famous personalities. In films, Eddie Murphy along with academy award winners Sidney Poiter, Denzel Washington, Jamie Foxx, Halle Berry, Forrest Whitaker and Morgan Freeman, Whoopi Goldberg and many others proved that it was possible for African Americans to reach the top in their professions.

In entertainment, musical recording studios led by Berry Gordy's Motown Records, Philadelphia International Records, Def Jam Records, Stax Records and many others issued an entire generation of inspirational music and era-defining records from their catalogues. Motown had an enormous influence of popular music and culture worldwide. Motown brought together a racially divided country and segregated society, around the world, touching people of all ages and races[cxxxiii] These are some

165

of the most important studios of all time and evoked an entire generation of music.

In literature, Toni Morrison, Maya Angelo and Alice Walker among others have been prominent in this field.

In business, fifteen African Americans became executives of "Fortune 500" largest companies in the United States.

However, despite achieving groundbreaking results and breaking glass ceilings that were unthinkable in previous decades, there are still many trailblazing efforts that need to be shattered so that they would later become the norm rather than the exception. Many factors have brought about change in the lives of African Americans. Some of the most important factors have been the impact of the second World War, the Civil Rights Movement under the leadership of Dr. Martin Luther King Jr., Civil Rights legislations in 1964 and 1965, and a more accepting attitude towards African Americans which has emerged since the 1970s in all sectors of the American society.

APARTHEID – SOUTH AFRICA

Apartheid was a system of legal racial segregation enforced by the National Party government of South Africa between 1948 and 1994. Apartheid had its roots in the history of Colonization and settlement of southern Africa with the development of practices and policies of separation along racial lines and domination by European settlers and their descendants. Following the general election of 1948, the National Party set in place its agenda of Apartheid, with the formalization and expansion of existing policies and practices into a system of institutionalized racism and white domination. Apartheid was dismantled in a series of negotiations from 1990 to 1993, culminating in elections in 1994, the first in South Africa with universal suffrage.

Apartheid legislation classified inhabitants and visitors into racial groups (black, white, colored, and Indian or Asian). South African blacks were stripped of their citizenship, legally becoming citizens of one of ten tribally based and nominally self-governing Bantustans (tribal homelands), four of which became nominally independent states. The homelands occupied relatively small and economically unproductive areas of the country. The government based the homelands on the territory of Black Reserves founded during the British Empire period, akin to the US Indian Reservation, Canadian First Nations reserves, or Australian aboriginal reserves. Many black South Africans, however, never resided in their identified "homelands". The homeland system disenfranchised black people residing in "white South Africa" by restricting their voting rights to their own identified black homeland. The government segregated education, medical care, and other public services; black people ended up with services greatly inferior to those of whites, and, to a lesser extent, to those of Indians and colored. The black education system was designed to prepare blacks for lives as a laboring class. There was a deliberate policy in "white South Africa" of making services for black people inferior to those of whites, to try to "encourage" black people to move into the black homelands.[cxxxiv]

Apartheid separated the races not only of whites from nonwhites, but also of nonwhites from each other, and, among the Africans (called Bantu in South Africa), of one group from another. In addition to the Africans, who constitute about 75% of the total population, those regarded as nonwhite include those people known in the country as Colored (people of mixed black, Malayan, and white descent) and Asian (mainly of Indian ancestry) populations.

Initial emphasis was on restoring the separation of races within the urban areas. A large segment of the Asian and Colored populations was forced to relocate out of so-called white areas. African townships that had been overtaken by (white) urban sprawl were demolished and their occupants removed to new townships well beyond city limits. Between the passage of the Group Areas Acts of 1950 and 1986, about 1.5 million Africans were forcibly removed from cities to rural reservations.

A combination of factors contributed to the end of Apartheid in South Africa. Many people point to the end of the apartheid as an illustration of what can happen when people from numerous governments and cultural backgrounds get together to oppose something whether it be institutionalized racism or war. It is also important to remember that although Apartheid is over in South Africa

One important factor in the end of Apartheid was pressure from inside the country. Members of the government began to have doubts about Apartheid, and several parties which were opposed to Apartheid also began to grow in South Africa, starting in the 1970s. Widespread opposition among both black and white South Africans to Apartheid policies essentially eroded Apartheid from within.

There was also a lot of external pressure, especially from Western nations, some of whom had extensive civil rights legislation. As the power of the Soviet Union began to decline, Western nations felt that Apartheid could no longer be tolerated, and they began to actively speak out against it. This period also marked moves toward democracy and self-determination in other African nations, as the West no longer feared the influence of Communism on recent African governments. Numerous diplomats and public officials made derisive comments about Apartheid, encouraging South Africa to bring it to an end.[cxxxv]

South Africa also experienced immense economic pressure to end Apartheid. Banks and investment firms withdrew from South Africa, indicating that they would not invest in the country until its institutionalized racism came to an end. Many churches also applied pressure. Combined with violent demonstrations from within and a mass organization of angry South Africans, these factors doomed Apartheid, and repeals to Apartheid laws started to occur in 1990; four years later, South Africa had a democratic election, and the last legal traces of apartheid were eliminated. The system finally collapsed due to international and Internal pressure led by Nelson Mandela.

The vestiges of Apartheid still shape and continues in South African politics and society. Likewise, in America, slavery ended well over a century ago, but the country is still experiencing pockets of racism, prejudices and discrimination in its society. Similar issues are occurring in South Africa. A lot of work still need to do to improve race relations in both countries.

THE HOLOCAUST

The Holocaust was the systematic, bureaucratic, state-sponsored persecution and murder of approximately six million Jews by the Nazi regime and its collaborators. The Holocaust was the period of oppression, incarceration, exploitation and annihilation that was initiated and executed by Nazi Germany and some other Axis countries against people of the Jewish race between 1939 and 1945. The perpetrators of the horrors that took place during the Holocaust were the Nazis and their allies. It was an agenda of systematic state sponsored murder of Jews led by Adolph Hitler's Nazi Party. The holocaust was the inhuman, genocide mass murder of approximately six million the Jews in German-occupied Europe during World War II.

German authorities also targeted other groups because of their perceived "racial inferiority": Roma (Gypsies), the disabled, and some of the Slavic peoples (Poles, Russians, and others). Other groups were persecuted on political, ideological, and behavioral grounds, among them Communists, Socialists, Jehovah's Witnesses, and homosexuals.

The Jews in Germany were subject to growing persecution by the Nazis since the latter came to power in 1933. From 1938 onwards, Hitler extended German control over a large part of Europe, especially after the invasion of Poland in 1939. In the process, the number of Jews under Nazi rule grew rapidly.

When the Germans invaded the Soviet Union in June 1941, special death squads (the "SD-Einsatzgruppen - mobile killing units") moved in and carried out mass open air killings of Jews, one of the most notorious being at Babi Yar where about 33,500 Jews were slaughtered.

In 1941-42 extermination camps were established by the Nazis in Poland. The following camps existed solely for exterminating usually by gassing and mass open air shootings.

Auschwitz (part of the Birkenau section)
Chelmno (Kolthoff)
Belzec
Sobador
Treblinka
Majdanek (part only; the rest was a very harsh concentration camp) * Maly Trostinets (in Belarus) * Bonney Gora (in Belarus)

Auschwitz became the most notorious camp of all. Part of it existed purely for the purpose of gassing victims. Others were worked to death on grossly inadequate food. There were frequent outbreaks of typhus in the labor camps. Some died from quack medical 'experiments'.

Two of Germany's Axis allies, Romania and the puppet state of Croatia, conducted their own Holocausts often using heavy, blunt instruments instead of gas. The Allies, though fighting against Germany, did not undertake any action designed specifically to stop the genocide. Over nine million Jews were sent to Concentration Camps where they were subjected to slave labor (many died from exhaustion or disease) or sent to gas chambers at extermination camps. Of these nine million approximately two thirds were killed.

The fate of displaced persons and Holocaust survivors was a major issue that eventually led to the establishment of Israel by Jewish survivors. The shock of this extermination campaign put a sharp decline to anti-Semitism around the world and even led to the creation of Israel to provide a permanent refuge from further persecutions. However, the conflicts with the Palestinians and some other Arabs are well documented. Many of the issues raised by this cataclysmic event continue to have an impact on our lives and the world in which we live.[cxxxvi]

UNITED STATES AND BRAZIL CURRENT RACIAL ISSUES

During the Transatlantic Slave Trade, more African slaves (4.9 million out of 12 million) went to Brazil than any place in the Americas with approximately thirty-five percent of the total. On the other hand, only about seven percent or approximately 450,000 African slaves went to the United States. Brazil was also the last Western hemisphere country to abolish slavery in 1888 whereas in the United States, slavery became illegal in 1865 when Congress passed the 13th Amendment to the Constitution.

The sheer weight of that many slaves during that time frame in both countries made them a larger part of both the American and Brazilian societies. In later decades, both countries dramatically increased their immigration patterns, mainly from European countries, to reflect the dominant culture. Today, about 54 percent of Brazilians are white, 39 percent are mixed race and 6 percent are black, according to the CIA World Factbook. Nearly half of all Brazilians are people of color. In the United States, blacks comprise 13 percent of the population with Non-Hispanics whites at 62 percent with Hispanics or Latinos at 18 percent and Asians at 6 percent of its total population.

In both countries, it is people of color who bear the brunt of that inequality. Brazilians of African descent earn 58 cents for every $1 a white Brazilian makes. The income gap between whites and people of African descent is nearly 2 to 1. Brazilians of African descent earn 58 cents for every $1 a white Brazilian makes, according to the government's National Household Survey. This in a country where one of every four Brazilians lives below the poverty level.

However, according to analysts and observers, Brazil's problems are social and economic and not racial, and many Brazilians don't think in racial terms. But that's not because blacks are considered inherently inferior, but because they haven't had the opportunities, analysts say. They believe the country really favors a meritocracy according to Larry Birns, director of the Council on Hemispheric Affairs, a liberal Washington think tank. If you had the talent and you had the education, you could succeed, it just so happened that most of the time the whites had the education.

Peter Hakim, president emeritus of the Inter-American Dialogue policy institute, notes that "if people move up the social ladder, they're not viewed by a racial prism." Much discrimination has been based on economic class, not race. They believe that it is a class and social issue that sometimes expresses itself as racial,

They admit that racism exists in Brazil but that there is not racial hatred. Still, though, people of color have faced barriers -- physical and otherwise. In the past, black people were required to use the service entrance to buildings.

About eight years ago, former Brazilian President Luiz Inacio Lula da Silva signed into law a widely debated measure that aims to end hundreds of years of racial disparity which is racialize the debate. It remains to be seen if the Racial Equality Law will succeed in a nation where about the half the population consists of people of color, but most of the political and economic power resides in white hands. Some observers say the law will just make matters worse because the inequalities are economic and social, not racial.

Senators removed provisions for racial quotas in universities and businesses, but the law offers tax incentives for enterprises that undertake racial inclusion according to the Globo newspaper. The law also defines what constitutes racial discrimination and inequality and says that anyone who considers himself or herself a black or mulatto is covered. In addition, the law stipulates that African and Brazilian black history be taught in all elementary and middle schools.

Observers emphasize it would be a mistake to compare the racial situation in Brazil with the United States. For starters, the definition of who is black is significantly different. In the United States, a person who has one drop of black blood is considered black. In Brazil, it's just the opposite. A person who has one drop of white blood is considered not black.

They also see a major difference in the aftermath in the two countries, though, because much of the racism in the United States was codified into laws that were not overturned until the federal Civil Rights Act of 1964 and the Voting Rights Act of 1965, one hundred years after the end of the Civil War. There were no Jim Crow laws in Brazil. There was prejudice, but it was not categorized in law. Brazil has a longer history of the two races living side by side.

They believe that compared with the United States, the difference between blacks and whites in Brazil was never that dramatic. As a result, there's a big difference in how African descendants see themselves in each country. Blacks in the United States recognize themselves mostly as being black first, but in Brazil, they see themselves as being black and Brazilian. Also, in the United States, race tends to be all-determining. It's not the same in Brazil. There's lots of discrimination, but not this all-too-determining factor.

They are wary that Brazil's new law could increase racial tensions because people could start thinking more in those terms. It's a very controversial measure because it mandates that people identify themselves as black or white and most Brazilians would have difficulties to put themselves in a category. Or the law could turn out to be meaningless and one of the things that could happen with it is nothing.

The law is one of a number of things that former President Lula done to face up to various Brazilian dilemmas. Brazil was very sensitive about race leading up to that point and now Brazil has begun to feel a little more relaxed about the whole thing. The law is significant because Brazil now is willing to admit racial discrimination.[cxxxvii]

Economically, Brazil is currently at a crossroad. When the Workers Party government came into power in 2003, the country redirected wealth towards those people who had been excluded in the past and the middle class grew from 35 percent to nearly 60 percent in a decade. In recent years, Brazil experienced some economic downfalls with commodity exports which fell sharply, its currency devalued by 30 percent and the governments, consumers and companies accumulated a lot of debt which brought on a recession. The resource rich country needs to diversify its economy and increase its trade options. The per capita income remains at just $8,700. As a result of the slowed economy, many citizens are protesting and demanding changes from the political and business establishments.[cxxxviii]

On the other hand, the United States economy has rebounded from the great 2008 recession. During the past six years, the nation has enjoyed a steady growth rate in most sectors of the economy and currently the country is experiencing historic low unemployment rates.

EUROPE AND UNITED STATES CURRENT RACIAL ISSUES

As the demographics of Europe and the United States change over the next century, so does the nature of those societies. America is expected to have an absolute non-white majority around 2045 and Europe is not far behind in the projections. This time however, unlike ancient Egypt, India or other civilizations or societies, there will be no new barbarians ready to take up the reins of Western civilization. There are no new territories to be developed or conquered on planet Earth. The last frontier left for consideration is space exploration.

In part two of this book on the formation of world orders, I discussed the causes that ended previous great empires, civilizations or societies and the time periods for their existence. Some of the reasons were issues dealing with over-expansion of their territory, multiculturalism, complacency, and inept leaders. The average time for their existence was 400 years which was the norm, but a few had survived for a millennium or more. The over-expansion of territories, the multicultural issues and immigration issues and poor leadership in both the United States and Europe will be examined.

The United States is a byproduct of the European's racial world order. The nation exists because it practically ridded the land of its indigenous people, expanded its territory by force and built the country with free labor from African slaves. This helped the nation achieve its status as the world's remaining superpower, particularly from an economic and military perspective. The continent of Australia and the country of Brazil basically followed the same model as the United States when European settlers conquer that country and replaced the native by genocide. Australia is presently not a world power but is a highly respected industrialized continent on a global scale.

OVER-EXPANSION

The European-American's racial world order is now over 400 years old. It is approaching the average shelf life for past great empires or civilizations. A notable difference with the European-American's world order versus other great civilizations were the size, nature and sheer scope of its territory. Although a few other empires covered a large land mass, the European-American's land mass was more comprehensive in scope and covered most of the world. It covered the continents of Africa, Australia, North America and South America and parts of Asia.

The current racial world order has many of the same issues which caused the demise of previous great civilizations, empires and societies. It may suffer the same fate if those critical issues are not addressed. As far as over expansion, after World War II, the European powers had to end their Colonization of their territories because of bankruptcy. However, today many European countries have rebounded from bankruptcy and continue to exert great influence over the former Colonies they occupied and newly created nations even today. The colonized countries around the world were finally granted their independence.

Likewise, countries such as Puerto Rico and the Virgin Islands are former Colonies of the United States have gained their independence but are still subsidized by the United States government. Moreover, since WWII, the United States expanded its military operation around the world in numerous key strategic locations. Although this is not a form of Colonization, the United States exerts great influence from both a political and economic standpoint in those areas. Even being the world's economic power, policing the world in this fashion must be a strain on the country's budget with so many other competing priorities that their citizens demand. However, the land and territories now occupied by the United States, Canada, Brazil and Australia, New

Zealand and other countries which were conquered by the Europeans from the indigenous populations during the existing world order. They have been formed as sovereign entities.

IMMIGRATION AND MULTICULTURAL ISSUES

Multicultural is another major issue that the United States and the continent of Europe are currently facing. In all the political entities, there is a strong sense of national identity based on racial, ethnic, gender and religious affinity. Multicultural is a complex issue with potential for both disaster and opportunity. The challenging of dealing with multicultural societies may be intensified due to a rapidly changing social landscape. It calls for open-mindedness to new ideas and a different way of doing things. It could leave to a journey of understanding and accepting others and offers a path to self-edification.

Europe, which has been grappling with a massive influx of refugees from the Middle East. Between 2015 and 2016, more than one million migrants and refugees came to the European Union. In America and Europe, capitalism thrives off the backs of immigrants who must accept menial labor for low wages. Industrialization succeeded because of a steady flow of immigrants who were not often able to collectively fight for better conditions. The United States' close proximity to the border of Mexico has resulted in legal and illegal immigrants from the country and other nearby Latin America countries. The immigration issue has been a very controversial issue in the United States for decades. It was during the Mexican American war during 1846 and 1848. Mexico believed that Texas was part of their territory and the United States believed it part of theirs. As a result, conflict broke out which led to the beginning of the war. America won the war and the Treaty of Guadalupe Hidalgo was established. According to the treaty Mexico had to not only give up Texas but also the "Mexican Territory" (now known as California, New Mexico, Arizona) This hotly debatable political issue has divided the country for decades to the extent that a comprehensive immigration bill has not been yet passed by the U.S. Congress.

Additionally, early America's original sin and centuries of brutal history and long legacy of slavery, segregation, Jim Crow laws, oppression and injustices against its African American citizens have made the multicultural issue problematic. The Civil Rights movement in the 1950s and 1960s led by Dr. Martin Luther King Jr. helped moved the country forward in race relations through legislation, judiciary and public policy initiatives. However, there is still a very deep divide among the various racial groups in how far the country has really advanced in race relations that still need to be resolved. Along with population estimates that by the year 2045, the nation may no longer have a majority white population. This has led to additional fear and anxiety by many citizens that may hamper the past progress made by the country in its quest for a just society for all of its citizens. The election of its first President of color, Barack Obama did not calm the racial tensions and fears in the country. In fact, it may have exacerbated race relations in views of political issues after his second presidential term expired. The country is undergoing continued growing pains and it will be interesting to see how events involving race relations unfold during the next few decades.

The continent of Europe is also experiencing multicultural issues. Humans have always practiced migration and vagility throughout the history of humankind. During the first world order, particularly in the nineteenth and twentieth centuries, migrants were flowing out of Europe to the Americas. Now the trend had been reversed and immigrants who have been forced out of their homeland for a variety of reason are going to nearby

Europe from the Middle East, Africa and Asia after America tighten its immigration laws. Globalization on the world market demands consumers and consumer cultures which help to create a more multicultural world. Many of the people who are forced into moving to American and European countries because their own countries have been ravaged and plundered by multi-national corporations, the International Monetary Funds (IMF), World Bank, and some trade agreements that reduced them to below poverty living conditions.

Unlike the United States, there are very few indigenous people on the continent of Europe. Europe's multicultural issue differ from America in that America looks at racial groups or ethnicity whereas Europe views cultural differences among those who have immigrated to various European countries. America, as a melting pot country was founded on a core set of values by its founders but still allowed its immigrants to value their cultural heritage. Europe, on the other hand, does not necessarily have a core set of values that it expects its immigrants to assimilate to. It fundamentally rejects that one value system is better than others and one group must adopt to the other one. This however has led to conflict because of historically fundamental dislikes that have existed among racial groups for centuries. Fear about the integrating of the new Muslim populations conflated with the issue of Islamic terrorism have created problems. Some immigrants could become legalized citizens but weren't allowed to emerge into the culture, thereby maintaining their cultures, identities and religions.[cxxxix]

Europe also has many countries that deal with immigrants differently based on its history, racial narrative and relations whereas America has States, but federal laws have trunked some state and local laws. At this time, the early consensus is that Europe has regarded multicultural as endangering their society, it has failed and there seems to be no option other than conflict between the racial groups.

There aren't even borders between most European nations anymore. It has become just one seamless continent. There isn't even a language barrier anymore. Almost all Europeans speak at least one or even several languages in addition to their native tongue. "It is possible, however, for subordinate group members to assimilate structurally, to a high degree, but still maintain ethnic group ties. There are, for example, Italian Americans who do not live in ethnic neighborhoods, who belongs to business organizations, who hold public office, and who socially primarily with dominant group members. These same people might also attend ethnic (Italian) weddings and funerals, eat pasta at least once a week, visit "Mama" on Sundays, and go to social functions sponsored by the Sons of Italy. If asked, however, many will say they are Americans, not Italian-Americans."[cxl]

The United States and Europe need to develop more comprehensive reform policies that are just and build societies that are both secure and welcoming, but immigration laws enforced with fairness and respect for human rights. The massive influx of new immigrant groups in the United States and Europe have destabilized specific concepts of race, led to a proliferation of identity position and challenged present modes of political and cultural norms.

GLOBAL LEADERSHIP

Poor and inept leadership of any civilization or society can ultimately lead to its demise. The moral weaknesses and incompetent of some recent leaders in the United States and some countries in Europe who has participated in events and activities that are not in the best interest of their sovereignties. In many cases, leaders elected by democracies reflect their populace. One can blame the people of the political entities for having elected such leaders, and it is the people who have suffered because of it, but it is an inherent feature of every democratic republic that the people can only vote on the basis of information the controlled media give them.

It is only in retrospect that a voter can know whether he has made a mistake. Some countries have gone to its ruin quietly and obediently, lacking a national leadership with the will to preserve the nation. The American people have likewise been saddled throughout its history with some treacherous leadership that has not served the best interests of the American people. Some of their leaders were weak-willed and self-indulgent people thoroughly not beholden to the best interests of American people but to external, internal forces or their own self-interests.[cxli]

It all depends on the leadership and political systems as to whether or not a society reign will be long lasting consequences. All societies, at some point in their history, will reach a point where their bad leaders take power. That is when they start to fall apart. Horrible leadership leads to corrupted system, and corrupted system, in turn, leads to anger and disloyalty of their own people, which marks the end of most societies.

PART SIX - ACHIEVING GLOBAL RACIAL JUSTICE AND SUSTAINABILITY

To achieve global racial sustainability and a better way of life for all the world's citizens will require major restructuring of all the world's institutions and systems, a sharing of power by all the racial groups, and an adjustment to the world's cultural values and lifestyles.

The driving force and passion that animate the racial groups at the bottom of society's racial social order are critically engaging the dominant cultures in contesting a wide range of long-established institutions and systems from education, health care, criminal justice, law, labor, economics, science, religion, politics to changing the perceptions of global racial justice. Issues of miseducation, segregation, poverty, exclusion, exploitation and other forms of injustice continue to disproportionally impact subordinate groups.

What is being seen globally is subordinate groups as a whole have not achieved the racial equality of the dominant culture, regardless of the level of development, region or type of economy. The global racial gap is narrowing but very slowly that it will take generations to correct. Global racial inequality is still the reality around the world and we are seeing that in all aspects of subordinate member's lives. Racial disparity still exists in economic opportunity, education, health and political empowerment. The world cannot afford to lose out of the skills, ideas and perspectives of subordinate groups. The equal contribution of all racial groups in this process of economic, political, cultural and societal transformation is critical.

While some of the world's societies have been more fluid with race relations than others, they have still maintained a global racial social order with Whites primary at the top, and African descent and indigenous people primarily at the bottom of the global social construct. As racism declined around the world, racial discrimination and inequalities, persisted, emerged, or changed forms in some societies more than others. For example, every modern society in the western hemisphere began as a white settler colony that seized indigenous land, marginalized (or eliminated) the original people, and forcibly imported African slave labor. These societies, despite some progress in race relations, unfortunately, still have the broad outlines of that arrangement as indicated by most group social indicators, including political power, educational level, wealth accumulation, collective economic power, incarceration rates and others. Subordinate groups are seeking the full equitable inclusion into the global society that they helped to shape, build and sustain.

AFRICA

The dismantling of the unequal world racial order would require making the continent of Africa whole again. From a global standpoint, Africa must be given central attention and is by far the major piece to the puzzle in restoring global racial parity and balance. Afterall, the Transatlantic Slave Trade started in Africa in the fifteenth century and this is the fitting place to where global racial justice should be sustained. Africa is the motherland to all the misplaced Africans who are dispersed around the world as well as the cradle and origin of all humankind and the history of civilization.

Although most of the countries in Africa gained their independence from European countries after World War II, they still are relying heavily on them economically for aid, charity, health and education matters. Coincidently, the Africa countries experience the same fate as the newly freed slave in the United

States when they achieved their freedom and independence. It was done in a haphazard manner with little resources given because most of the European countries were in bankruptcy after World War II. The hasty and poorly planned European exit from Africa led to some tenuous country borders and governments, planting the seeds for many of the conflicts seen today.^{cxlii} Likewise, in the United States, the freed slaves were not given their 'forty acres and a mule' and adequate resources to survive in their new realities. In Africa's case, this in turn led to some inept leaders who took advantage of the convoluted run countries that they are still experiencing today. In some instances, the foreign countries help armed and defended some the dictators who reaped atrocities on their own people.

Africa is a huge continent in land mass, the second largest in the world. It is one of the fastest growing and has the youngest populations in the world with huge wealth, tremendous resources and minerals. Also, the countries in Africa are some of the youngest ones in the world as far as achieving their independence compared to many other world's countries. Many of the Africa countries became independent from European rule after World War II.

Africa does not need to be nurtured by the same foreign countries who occupied and exploited the continent of its wealth for centuries and helped caused its current instability and current social ills. When they do attempt to offer solutions, they are usually self-serving. The Europeans powers took no measures to help transition Africa and many of the colonized countries around the world to self-governance after World War II. Consequently, Africa was not prepared for a modern economy that would benefit from industrialization and was plunged into a primarily subsistence farming economy. Because of the authentic political experiences, African leaders were not equipped to govern after they achieved their independence. This plunge Africa into poverty and civil war.[cxliii] Unfortunately, this scenario was played out with many of the other Colonized countries around the world.

The continent of Africa has the sustainable resources to sustain herself and should break away from dependency on foreign aid. The foreign countries should leave the countries in Africa alone to make their own decisions. In recent years, Africa has produced some intelligent and competent people who can independently critically analyze its problems and issues and come to applicable decisions to govern and maintain themselves.

In recent decades, many of the African countries' best and brightest students have gone to some of the finest educational institutions around the world since the end of the European's Colonization after World War II. Many have brought back those academic principles and concepts back home to implement them in their societies and govern their populace. For example, census data shows Nigeria immigrants have the highest levels of educational obtainment in the United States (U.S.), far outpacing whites in Asians. Many members of the African countries are obsessed with obtaining bachelors and post graduate degrees in the technical and sciences field.[cxliv] In addition, sub-Saharan immigrants in the United States are often more educated than those in top European destinations, including the United Kingdom (UK), France, Italy and Portugal. In the U.S., 69% of sub-Saharan immigrants had at some college experience compared to the UK at 49%, while it was lower in France (30%), Portugal (27%) and Italy (10%).[cxlv]

In the past few decades and centuries, the masses of African people have not had these opportunities. This type of academic excellence bodes well with the future of many African countries in the upcoming decades if they continue the pursuits in these areas.

It is possible for world societies to change their institutions and move onto better development paths although it is not of course inevitable that they will do so. There are numerous examples around the world. For example, Japan, Thailand and Singapore were also poor and underdeveloped during this period and they are more prosperous than Africa today. The European Colonization did bring some proximate benefits in terms of technology and access to implantation of modern institutions. Yet little attempt was really made to make such benefit endure and many were restricted to the Colonial period. The Europeans also brought racism, discrimination, inequality and seriously warped many African political and economic institutions. Once the European powers left, much of what was positive was short-lived and went it reverse while many of the negatives returned and endured.[cxlvi]

Globalism is impacting all countries/continents around the world from the highly developed ones such as the United States, Norway, Sweden, Canada, New Zealand, Switzerland, the Netherlands, Germany, Singapore, Denmark to the resource-rich countries such as Saudi Arabia, Russia, Brazil, South Africa, Venezuela, Nigeria and other non-resource rich developing countries.

During the past twenty-five years, South Africa, Nigeria, Egypt, Saudi Arabia, Brazil, Mexico, Venezuela, Turkey, Russia, Indonesia, India and China have undergone enormous changes and their fate will determine the future of the twenty-first century global economy. These are twelve of the world's largest and most important developing counties. Three of these countries, South Africa, Nigeria and Egypt, are located in the continent of Africa. Each will be considered below.

South Africa has not maintained its positive momentum and legacy that former Presidents Nelson Mandela and Thabo Mbeki provided the country after Apartheid fell. Economically, it now remains one of the most unequal societies in the world in per capita income among the country's elite and average citizens. There is chronic poverty and joblessness and some of its weaknesses come from falling global demand for the commodities it exports and the continued legacy of Apartheid that affect the townships and under-developed rural areas that continue to separate the poor people chance to learn and work. There is also chronic corruption and poor leadership from the African National Congress (ANC). That is now changing as challenges to the ANC with the moderate Democratic Alliance and the Economic Freedom Fighters and others have won control of many government elections in recent years, so the tide may be turning in the future.

Like South Africa, Nigeria has an increasingly unequal society. It is Africa's most populous country and its largest economy. It also has a major problem with inequalities between the haves and the have nots. In recent years, despite Nigeria's economy growing at a strong pace, people living in poverty have increased and the distribution of wealth and income have increased significantly. Another major problem that divides the country is its religious affiliations. Christians are located in the country's southern states and the underdeveloped Muslims-dominated north. Leaders in both regions struck up an informal deal to rotate the country's President but it has not worked out smoothly as planned as slowed economic growth and high unemployment curtailed the plan. Nigeria is heavily dependent on oil as an OPEC member, but it needs to diversify its economy from heavily dependent on oil exports.

Similar to South Africa and Nigeria, Egypt too has a problem with inequality with nearly 30 percent of its population living in poverty. This problem has created some resistance and uprising during the past few years with terrorist attacks. Egypt had sought financial help from countries such as Saudi Arabia and other Persian Gulf states, but lower oil prices have curtailed that assistance. Also, Egypt has a political structure in which the military can overrule the civilian government in decisions involving its political and economic privileges. One of Egypt's greatest challenges will be its exploding population which is expected to double from 2000 to 2050. This population growth is expected to leave less room for agriculture growth, and food and water shortages. This has led to discontentment among its growing young population who blame their government and the International Monetary Fund (IMF), an institution that identify with globalism, which insists on state spending cuts in exchange for its loans.

The nature of South Africa, Nigeria and Egypt's economies and the limitations of their politics make them particular vulnerable. These countries have issues with the pace and scale of technological change in the workplace. There is some vulnerability to automation, its disruptive affects and the nation's capacity to respond to it. In the near future, it remains to be seen if these African countries and others have the political will, money and foresight to adapt their citizens to rapid technological changes that will determine whether they survive or thrive.cxlvii

Gaining independence to governed themselves and making their own decision and destiny is the key step for any society. Africa has not had that opportunity during the past five centuries. The world has changed dramatically during that time economically, politically, socially and technologically. Before the two World Wars, Africa was dependence on European Colonial powers. Also, the world has changed since the nineteenth and early twentieth century when multiple great powers cooperated and competed on a global scale.

The world is even different today after World War II when the United States emerged as the world's dominant power. Due to globalization, the world is more interconnected more than ever before. The various social media networks and media sharing sites have allowed instant flowing of information and ideas. They also allow endless possibilities for education, partnerships and commercialism. However, the issues facing the world are more challenging and complex, but the global powers are more dispersed.

Now is the opportunity for the continent of Africa to rejoin the many nations and continents around the world to find their niche in the global economy. Africa should be given that chance to join the world's community as an equal partner in many of the global governance institutions such as the UN, NATO, G7, G20, IMF, World Bank, WTO, WHO, UNHCR who are dominated by the West.[cxlviii] Like all countries and continents, Africa exists in a global economy world. There need to be closer relationships between Africa and the West and strength their position with the East. Africa should be part of the global community and able to engage in regional and international summits, partnerships, and trade agreements in good faith with other world's countries. However, the Africa Union should wisely choose and charter its future path based on its past history and current needs. The path taken by Africa and its countries could be independence and cooperation with other countries or global governance, control and domination.

Africa should also strengthen its position with the International Monetary Funds (IMF) - (loans for countries in crisis), the World Bank (loans for developing countries) and push for free markets and trade across the globe. However, the goal for most African countries should be to borrow only as needed and make good use of the funds that are available. They must understand the terms and agreements of their loans as they can place a heavy burden on the countries and their citizens. The IMF and World Bank today have a strong influence over economic policies in many countries. The inability of many countries to repay their debt has made them dependent on new loans. Reforming of these institutions are needed to create incentives for countries to increase economic freedom. Because the work of these institutions deters economic freedom, the vast majority of recipient countries have been unable to develop fully after over 60 years of independence.

In recent decades, many African countries have made trade deals with China involving major loans and aid. Likewise, the countries in Africa needs to understand the clauses and conditions of those loans because in many cases, they are not revealed to the public. A few African countries are already indebted to China.[cxlix] However, the overwhelming majority of all debts of African countries are owed to Western institutions such as IMF, the World Bank, IDB Bank and others. Presently, China's investment in the recent economic development in Africa is the driving force behind Africa's current level of economic growth. Yet, Africa needs to be careful with this issue and draw lessons from its historical experiences. Sometimes a trading partner(s) may be self-serving and not have Africa's best interest. Africa needs to select forward thinking leaders who are able to negotiate the best deals possible for its populace which will serve the best interest of the continent in the future.

Presently, Africa plays a minor part of the world's agenda. The dominant world cultures make these decisions and set the world's agenda and basically determine what is discussed on the word's stage. Unfortunately, countries in the continent of Africa have not been a major part of their agenda. Ironically, race has never been a major topic when the dominant cultures meet to discuss the world's agenda. In major global agreements, the countries of Africa are not offered seats at the table. The world's leadership is in denial of how race have played in major role in the many past and present racial inequalities that exist around the world since the fifteenth century. They also may not be inclined to share power with other world cultures and want to protect their brand.

This will require some ingenuities, accountability and creative thinking by the African Union, its leaders and their citizens to carve their own niche on the world stage. Their leaders and people must unite, break the stranglehold from other foreign countries, their handouts and truly become an independent and political autonomy entities capable of governing their people with autonomous economic development policies. The Africa leaders and people need to determine their destiny and charter a path about how they can develop the nations themselves.

Africa should engage more heavily in entities outside the big multilateral institutions in which they currently do not play a prominent role and consider regional organizations, private sector groups, foundations, civil society groups, etc. Many of them operate outside the control of global inter-governmental organizations, yet it will allow Africa the freedom and independence needed to pursue activities in their best interest that may allow some equitable to the traditional global institutions.

If the history of the last six decades since 1960 when multiple African countries gained their independence from European powers is an indication of what is to come, the continent of African will continue to fight against outside Western intervention and strive to determine the destiny of the continent's people based on their own national and class interests. If they can do this over the next few decades, the dominant cultures will have no choice but to bring them into the world's fold as equal partners on the global stage.

STRATEGIES FOR ACHIEVING GLOBAL RACIAL JUSTICE AND SUSTAINABILITY

The number one strategy for achieving global racial sustainability obviously is to make the continent of Africa whole again. However, many people in the subordinate groups of the global racial order are dispersed throughout the world in all the countries and continents. Racism will never be eliminated and eradicated in the world but over time cultures can be changed and be amendable to others with different genetic makeups and lineages. Humankind can evolve where this behavior will not be the norm and an acceptable form of behavior that has led to many atrocities throughout human history.

The solution to global racial sustainability and justice is multi-variable and will require several problematic solution paths. These complex issues developed over several centuries, some progress have been made as mentioned earlier but plenty of resolved issues remain. A major issue is the perceptions by different racial groups of how far we have come in resolving our global racial issues. Presently, how some members of the dominant and subordinate groups view racial issues in our global society come to starkly different conclusions. Understanding how race and inequalities (listed in part four) play a role in past and present world's events and issues and how racial groups reach conclusions about them is crucial in making progress on them. Understanding the history of race relations from a global perspective is critical for all racial groups so that appropriate strategies can be developed.

Hopefully, the information in this book has placed all the major world's events and issues during the existing world racial order in an historical sequential order with a new perspective. In our quest to provide strategies, we must deal with the present issues and their future but be mindful of how past events played a major role in creating them.

In the ongoing world's debate of achieving global racial justice among all racial groups that is particularly superimposed in pluralistic societies, there have been two main prevailing solutions on the current plight of subordinate groups on the lower end of the world's racial order.

Generally, one thought is to blame the dominant culture who created these social ills beginning with the Transatlantic Slave Trade in the fifteenth century. It is based on the premise that before any member of the subordinate group made a single choice to direct their life, the choices of the dominant culture that currently rule this world predetermines the scope and nature of their individual choices. The fifteenth century's Transatlantic Trade Slave and its aftermath limited members and descendants of the subordinate groups from reaching their full potentials. It is a belief that their destiny has already been predetermined and shaped even before members of the subordinate groups were born. It is based on the premise that members of the subordinate group's existential reality were shaped by the context and standards of the dominant culture. Basically, the deck of life is stacked against them and no matter what strategies they come up with, it will not change their fate. The philosophy of 'pulling yourself up by your bootstrap' is false and could result in anti-social behaviors.

The other prevailing thought is the world is now a more just society, there are not any barriers preventing subordinate groups from reaching their full potential and it's up to them to solve their problems and issues. It is based on the premise that at some point, subordinate groups must take full responsibilities for their actions despite their lot in life and deal with them accordingly.

Whatever the views, it is not quite that simple. Change in the status quo is not instant and sometimes not obvious and does not necessarily happen in our lifetimes. Nor those it includes the change some people may want to see. The dominant culture will not simply give up their wealth and status and share power with the subordinate groups. However, change will certainly not happen if the subordinate groups do nothing. One still must take accountability and responsibility for their actions or else they will not get the change that they want. Perhaps a social evolutionary view should be taken. Similarly, social evolution is not too much differently than a biological evolution in that both take a long time. Oftentimes with changes going unnoticed in real time and are jumpstarted by revolutions.

We are dealing with some extremely complex societal issues that are very far reaching in scope that took centuries to develop and it will take time for them to be dismantled. Strides have been taken during the past century but there are still plenty of unresolved racial issues. Some past and present racial inequalities are listed in part four. There is accountability with both viewpoints. This book has presented an accurate portrayal of the world's dilemma from the beginning of the existing world racial order in the fifteenth century to this point in our world's history. Now we as a global community must take the next step in changing our institutions, systems and cultural behaviors to ensure that the present inequalities and stereotypes based solely on one attribute of a person's genetic makeup and lineage are properly addressed.

SUBORDINATE GROUP STRATEGIES

The legacy of slavery and worldwide Colonialism are still very relevant today because some dominant group members and ancestors passed down a culture and beliefs from perpetual generations to their descendants in many parts of the world. Some of their descendants end up developing implicit or unconscious and even intentional biases and race-based associations in all walks of their lives. Some members of the dominant group are still uncomfortable talking about slavery and worldwide Colonialism, its aftermath and prefer not to discuss it openly.

This lack of acknowledgement is a major problem. Slavery and Colonialism and its aftermath perpetuated the myths that some subordinate group members were worthless and demeaning. As a result, some subordinate members developed a very poor perception of themselves and have little or no self-esteem. This along with the numerous barriers and inequalities that were placed in front in them which are listed in part four after the Transatlantic Slave Trade led generations of some subordinate group members to engage in self-destructive acts and anti-social behaviors. Some felt that their life choices and success were limited and capped by a dominant society that in essence treated them as global second-class citizens.

The culture and environment play a huge role and have a major impact in the development of one's life. However, it should not be a necessary conclusion that their culture or environment impedes development, accomplishments, or success. Even growing up in a racist environment, while troubling, disturbing, and sometimes fatal, is no excuse for not seeking the most from their existence. Despite these setbacks, it is still not a reason to quit. Subordinate group members must somehow muster through these obstacles to gain a strong balance of self-confidence, self-respect and self-knowledge. Subordinate group members must keep striving until they reach the fullness of their potentials.

Subordinate group member's ancestors were creative and industrial people who paved the way for their descendants and subordinate group members need to start taking some risks and start believing in themselves as individuals and as a group. Avoidance is not a wise path and is not an option. Their survival depends on proactive measures. It is in their nature to survive. This strong desire is what made their ancestor's existence so meaningful and their legacy should serve as a blueprint for their descendants in the future.

The reality that racism still exists is no cause for the subordinate group members to not seek success. The subordinate group member's level of attainment should not be artificially capped by some members of the dominant culture. Also, one should not allow themselves to engage in anti-social behaviors by letting their life be defined by some descendants of the dominate culture. Despite the historical reasons for their current existence, it then becomes ostensibly a self-fulfilling prophecy propagated by racist myths.

Responsibility and accountability are not functioning of skin color. Values are not color dependent. Hope, dreams and aspirations are not reserved only for member of the dominant culture. It should not be an overarching reach that somehow subordinate group's success and destiny were shaped before they were born and predetermined by some members of the dominant culture. Also, they should not allow their hopes, dreams, aspirations and success to be stifled by their circumstances and environment. Members of subordinate groups should believe that they are in control of their fate and destiny. They must keep believing in themselves.

Instilling personal responsibility in someone, particular at early ages helps drive the difference in their successes and failures in life and is critical among all racial group. Today, there appears to be a lack of hunger, desire and passion in some people. Maybe the lack of personal hardships dealing with the toils and strifes of life that the previous generations experience may have something to do with it. Subordinate members in this generation face a different set of challenges than their ancestors in previous generations. Today, the world is very different, transformed by the digital revolution and advances in medicine and human knowledge. It is important that they adapt to these changes and be prepared to deal with the challenges and obstacles that they will face by educating and preparing themselves.

Subordinate group members must learn about their ethic group that contributes to the inferiority complex that some experience. This includes acknowledging and embracing a positive sense of identity and self-worth. They should read and understand their cultural history and visit cultural museums to gain a better sense of self-identity. Teaching subordinate group members about their roots and addressing the racial issues can propel them toward individual and group progress. Perhaps what is needed from subordinate group members of African descent is an "ethnic resurgence from the 1970s in which a degree of improved self-esteem and identification with Africa" was manifested.[cl] A sustained cultural revival from perpetual generations must be maintained to help subordinate group member in their quest for the truth.

Parental guardians and role models need to continue to instill belief, confidence and work ethics in their children. They must teach their children to be the very best they can be, knowing that they will never be perfect individuals but in the effort to be the best, they can maximize their abilities and reach their potentials. Furthermore, subordinate group members must learn to think critically and analytically in problem solving and break away from the concepts of charity, self-dependency and the propaganda that have been instilled on the subordinate groups by the dominant culture during the past five centuries. The personal choices of subordinate group members will be critical in determining how global racial justice is redefined in decades to come.

Subordinate group members need to critically examine the conditions of the dominant culture that has been forced and opposed upon him during the past five centuries. They need to re-orientate their religion, education, values, culture, heritages and identities that were thrust upon them and are still causing many of the social ills that still exist today. They need to critically analyze these manifestations to see if they serve their best interests and adjust as needed. Many subordinate members have been miseducated by the dominant culture in their role in society at large. After analyzing these conditions and facts, proactive steps should be taken to plan and deal with them accordingly. This effort will allow them to find their niche in our global society.

Unfortunately, there is not a 'cook book' approach, or a 'one stop shop' in dealing with one's life plan. Like all people, subordinate group members are very diverse individuals with different life's goals, priorities, needs, abilities, potentials and visions. Individuals must make a good faith effort to execute their plans that would be tailored to their lots in life. However, the can use a 'best practice' approach that will offer ideas that represent the most efficient or prudent course of action.

African Americans were brought to the Americas as slaves, stripped of their cultural heritage and forced to adapt and acculturate to the dominant culture beginning at levels far below those of typical immigrants. The dominant culture purposefully revise history, obfuscate subordinate members accomplishments, devalues members of the subordinate groups and perpetuate a system that serve to subjugate rather that uplift. The impacts of racism that they experience are far-reaching and have long lasting consequences. But it is still not an excuse to not achieve. African Americans should be proud of their glorious past history in Africa that Europeans and Americans tried to hide from the world during the past five centuries to justify the past and present oppression of the subordinate groups. African Americans must not languish in their current state of affairs. They must present their side of the story to the world and continue the tradition of their ancestors with full confidence and hope that things will improve in the future.

Many opportunities that exist today were not possible to African American's ancestors during slavery or even before the civil rights movement in the 1950's and 1960's. Also, opportunities were not possible for the victims of the South African's Apartheid, the Holocaust and many other atrocities around the world. This is not a denial of any accomplishments during the past few decades but the acknowledgement of their inadequacies. Some global societal gains and transformational events during the past few decades have made this possible in some areas of the world even with present barriers still in place. Global racism toward subordinate groups is less blatant today, but subordinate group members still do not have the same level of status as the dominant racial groups. Implicit, unconscious and even intentional bias is still very much present in societies that affect people lives in voting rights, access to education, employment, treatment by law enforcement and the criminal justice system.

It starts with individuals and families stepping up and facing the harsh reality of their situation. They must make tough decisions and recognize that in the current environment, success comes with supreme effort and sacrifice. Unfortunate, not everyone will make it and not all will rise but nature never meant it that way. However, over time the subordinate groups will get better. But they can't give up for the sake of their children and their children's children. In the grand scheme of things, people are here just for a moment. They need to see the big picture in the long run because we are living in the present. Even in the present times, a lot of individuals have made it but not the subordinate groups as a whole.

We are presently living during global racial transformation and change but unfortunately it is still going to take some time. We cannot undo five centuries of racism, discrimination, bigotry, slavery, colonization, Apartheid, Holocaust, segregation, and total domination of subordinate groups worldwide by the dominant culture that was based solely on one attribute of a person's genetic makeup and lineage and expect society to change dramatically even in a few decades. Racism will never be fully eradicated, but things can get better in the next few decades.

DOMINANT GROUP STRATEGIES

Dominant group members can play a key role in the effort to balance past and present global racial inequities. In part four under Identifying Past and Present Global Racial Inequalities, numerous inequalities are listed. This clearly shows that many government entities around the world through their politics, public policies, legislation, laws, norms, customs, institutions and systems have placed subordinate groups in the position they are in today. There is no doubt that these systems and institutions have been complicit in constructing and perpetuating these global inequalities. There were a lot of societal shaping factors at play that need to be reshaped or unshaped. A clean blank slate for all racial groups at this point in world's history is not workable due to prior horrific actions and atrocities which resulted in the enormous economic, social, political and cultural disparities that exist today. These governmental entities owe subordinate groups some relief to address and undo past racial injustices and the present barriers that still exist today. Accountability of the dominant culture is needed due to intangible social and political forces that have recently been at play. But rather than turn from it, this might be an opportunity to confront these systematic and pervasive inequalities with rectitude.

The education of all of its citizens of real-world history should be one of the key cornerstones for any society and culture. There is no doubt that Europe and the United States have fallen short in this effort with the suppression of African's creative excellence.

The dominant culture has purposefully revise history during the past five centuries to maintain their power and privileges by obfuscating the accomplishments of subordinate groups, particular Africans. Generally, at different educational levels in America and Europe, you can easily find classes in ancient, mediaeval Europe thought and Greek philosophy. Very seldom will you find courses that deal with courses in ancient, mediaeval and modern Africa unless they are available in the Black Studies departments at Universities around the world in which only a small percentage of students take the classes.

The dominant culture has purposely ignored the history and culture of subordinate groups and nations. The accomplishments of the Mesopotamia, Greece and Rome are regularly taught in educational institutions around the world but the ancient African Kingdoms such as Songhay Empire, Ethiopia and Egypt are generally omitted. Much of the early civilizations of the Mediterranean world was decidedly influence by Africans.[cli] The dominant culture presently controls most of the world's systems and institutions as well as the world's media. It is important that real world history be told to all world's citizens. This acknowledgement will allow future generations to deal with racial issues more openly and honestly than what has happened during the past five centuries under the existing world racial order.

Europe and America are well aware of this history because they enslaved and colonized all the African countries except Ethiopian for centuries and stole and pillage a large portion of their wealth, artworks and artifacts. When some of the courses are offered in the school systems, the historical accuracy is watered down that they omit critical key portions of what really happened in the world's events. Many countries around the world, including America, Canada. The Netherland, Ireland and the United Kingdom have celebrated February or October as 'Black History' month for recognizing the history accomplishments of Africans and African Americans but there is no substitution for teaching accurate information on Africa and world history that should be available in their educational systems on a large scale. African history is a prominent part of America and world history due to the Transatlantic Slave Trade and the colonization of Africa by the European powers for centuries. More importantly, the origin of mankind started in Africa. Africa is the cradle of civilization.

In a pluralistic society when the dominant cultures control all the major institutions and systems, the sustainability of the subordinate group is critical as their welfare impacts the entire community. To see new economic growth for the subordinate groups and deal with their socioeconomics issues such as poverty and crime, creating higher paying jobs and providing educational opportunities or creating a positive environment for establishing small businesses are critical and essential elements in moving the community forward. The dominant culture must realize that the subordinate groups basically want the same things they want for themselves and their families. The government entities and other stakeholders should consult with the subordinate community when developing new programs that will affect their communities. If the dominant group is sincere in their efforts, they must not only advise the subordinate groups what they plan to do but invite them to the table in good faith when discussions and decisions are made so they can be an integral part in those group power discussions. They must also ensure that the multicultural diversity within their jurisdictions be reflected in their appointment to boards, commissions and committees.

Some dominant group members wish to cultivate strong relationships with subordinate group member in eradicating racism and becoming allies in the fight against racial inequalities. Unfortunately, as mentioned above, there isn't extensive education in the world that examine global racism throughout history. As a result, there are not nearly enough opportunities for dominant group members to learn how they can bridge gaps of misunderstanding, distrust and guilt toward achieving true equity and inclusion for subordinate groups. For too long, dominant group members have only heard about racism in the context of what not to do, but rarely, do they hear about how they can be proactive in this area.[clii]Members of the dominant culture will never have the same understanding or broad range of experiences that subordinate group members have but they can still join the conversation and become allies for global racial justice.

Enlightened members of the dominant cultures should also speak to lesser enlightened group members about their intentional, implicit and subconscious biases. The power of culture and attitudes cannot be denied in our social realities. It shapes us, but we must shape it. Many members of the dominant culture grew up in homogenous white environments. Some remains coddle in the ignorance of subordinate groups and that shield their dominant culture homogeneity. The recent racial transformation events around the world added to the complexity of their world with demands from the subordinate groups. Ruminants of the world's past cultural ideology where overt racism reign supreme, its history was ignored, and subordinate group voices were not heard is a dying ideology. When confronted with new racial awareness, their old inclinations that rely on their homogeneous upbringing and environment, make some of them wholly inadequate to deal with their new realities. The enlightened dominant group members can educate their fellow members in our increase complex, tense and racially fraught climate. Because individual behavior is shaped and promoted by dominant culture and practice, he must be part of the individual-level change process.

Enlightened members of the dominant culture must challenge racist attitudes in their family members, circle of friends, workplace and all walks of life. The offending party is probably going to be more open to hearing from someone who presently shares a similar culture. While most members may not consciously and actively try to be racists, some may be conditioned into racism from their culture and environment in which they are not even aware of.

The subordinate groups do not have access to these people in the same manner that dominant group members. They are not responsible for the way the dominant culture thinks and feel about them and cannot change their attitudes and behaviors. Nor is it their responsibility to soothe the dominant culture's race-based fears. And it is not the responsibility of subordinate group members to educate the dominant culture about race. When members of the dominant culture speak, they have more influence over other members in their culture than a subordinate group member and unfortunately, they are more likely to be believed. Historically, perspectives and voices from dominant group members have been given priority over the lived experiences and knowledge of subordinate group members.

The dominant group members may not have committed the sins of their ancestors, but they surely have inherited its benefits. As members of the dominant group, they benefit directly from racism based solely on the color of their skin which is an unearned advantage privilege. Even if they have never contributed to biases or prejudice against subordinate group members, it is still in their best interest to help find remedies for it because it may travel to their existence at some point.

COMMUNITY BUILDING STRATEGIES

Another key strategy for achieving racial justice is community building. It can include subordinate group members who was born, raised and nurtured in the marginalized communities but left at some point in their lives due to lack of opportunities. In some cases, they were practically driven away from those communities due to socioeconomic conditions. Some left to pursue opportunities in various fields of endeavor and became successful. But they left behind family relatives, childhood friends and long-term neighbors who were not able to leave. Over a period of time, due to socioeconomic conditions, those marginalized communities deteriorated even further. That in turn splinters families and concentrates long-term joblessness, poverty and a rather logical but dangerous degree of hopelessness in those communities.

It is very easy for subordinate group members to stay away from their former communities and not get involved. But there are young people in their former communities that need to hear their story and seek guidance from them for their personal inspiration. The knowledge that they gained over the years while they were away from their native community can serve and edify it. Everyone has different circumstances but those who are able to give back to their communities should do so in some fashion. They should remember that the subordinate group members they left behind in those marginalized communities are still the victims of the same system that cause them to leave in the first place for better opportunities and a better way of life.

Community building strategies involve individuals, local governments, universities, private companies and other organizations and stakeholders taking responsibility for eradicating racism in their jurisdictions. This will instill trust, harmony and cooperation among all racial groups. The departure of jobs, shortfalls in housing, transportation problems, and other concerns in subordinate communities are influenced mainly by regional actions that are forced upon these communities. Those measures can be resolved to some degree by community leaders, local non-profits, and faith-based partners coming together as a network to create strategic planning plans and goals that will that will compel city, county, and regional leaders to include them in decision-making planning which will ensure effective implementation of needed programs in their neighborhoods and communities.

People who participate in decision-making that affects their communities feel a higher degree of ownership and commitment to the planning process. When residents of subordinate communities are involved in the planning process, the quality of output is higher than if they were not included. However, the percentage of community residents who are involved directly involved in the planning is usually small. As a result, community planners must find ways to communicate with the entire community as much as possible. This can be assured by enlightening them with information related to the planning process and making sure they are engaged to some degree. This will cause a greater percentage to remain engaged. Trust must also be established. This can be achieved when subordinate stakeholders feel they are listened to and shown respect.

It is imperative that community organizations in subordinate cultures find ways to work with neighborhood businesses, as well as national and local corporations to sponsor neighborhood improvement initiatives and needs. The organizational leaders must understand and recognize that businesses and corporate partners do not have enough understanding of the needs of the community. As a result, the planning process must be comprehensive and informative. Importantly, it must fit into the funding goals of the business stakeholders as much as possible.

It is vitally important that the media portrayal of subordinate members improve in local communities. Presently a negative portrayal of subordinate groups involves excessive coverage on account of criminal activities and socioeconomic conditions which create very negative images in subordinate communities. It also influences negative treatment of subordinate groups in the criminal justice system and society at large by the dominant culture. With limited amounts of subordinate members portrayed in the media, it might be the only exposure some people see for an entire group of people.

Media coverage, television programs and public service announcement that spotlight the achievement of subordinate groups will have a positive effect for the communities they live and work in. Likewise, the regional and national media need to improve their coverages concerning race. The subordinate communities should be encouraged to promote a positive image of its members by documenting and disseminating information on its success and contribution in the development of the overall community. Media plays into race relations and can affect the perception of a subordinate member's racial group.

A solution to global racism is for all racial groups is to recognize racism in your communities by embracing it even with all its problems. Community forums with listening skills sessions can be developed by bringing together a broad section of society to speak openly and honestly about race relations, experiences and realities of all of its members. Educating others on how other member's culture can be a step inclusion and preventing the marginalization of subordinate groups. This would be an opportunity to promote cultural awareness which will highlight anti-racism and promote healthy group relationship activities. This may create some transformational events and activities at the local level that can help shape and redefine the future of its communities in upcoming decades.

SUBORDINATE OWNED BUSINESSES STRATEGIES

Creating and maintaining businesses and entrepreneurship is another key cornerstone for any stable community and society. Entrepreneurship is a viable and necessary option for creating economic and civic prosperity or that group will forever be marginalized. It will allow members of the subordinate groups the independence and freedom they need to become self-sufficient and control their own destiny. It would allow them to own their businesses and not depend and rely on other racial groups to make a living and determine their future destiny.

During Reconstruction and post Reconstruction prior to the Civil Rights movement in the 1950's and 1960's, there were numerous prosperous thriving businesses in the black communities. After the Civil Rights movement, legal segregation ended in the United States, more black people were able to get an education or pursue other interests. Many became part of the Great Migration to the large cities in the North and Midwest to work in manufacturing jobs or trades. The global economy and other factors caused many factories to close down so the black workforce took a large hit. While there was a steady rise in black businesses in the 90s, it wasn't enough to offset those who lost their jobs.

One of the goals of Dr. Martin Luther King Jr. and the civil rights movement was an advocation of desegregation but not to the detriment or expense of integrating subordinate groups out of economic power. Subordinate owned businesses must be brought back to the marginalized communities around the world in sufficient numbers to meet the demands of their communities.

The lack of subordinate owned business in marginalized communities in the United States and around the world is a major problem. When businesses are present even in predominately black and brown countries around the world, they are owned by

Korean, Asians, Indians, or other foreign cultures. In the United States, national and international businesses refuse to open stores, restaurants, banks and shops in marginalized communities because it doesn't fit their business plan.

Entrepreneurship was started by our ancestors after the Civil war during Reconstruction but pushback by the dominant culture in recent decades slowed its growth. The foundation of generational business prosperity that was built by previous generations suffered a setback, but it has not been fatal. The foundation of entrepreneurship is the combination of values and education. While not necessarily sufficient conditions, they are necessary ones. The values and education require a mindset change in the subordinate group and require future generations to effectively lay the foundation. Now a new generation of entrepreneurship will have to take the mantle for succeeding generations to lay a new foundation. I believe if entrepreneurship becomes a priority again, we can reenact more Tulsa Wall streets in the world which start with education or symposium workshops.

The lack of knowledge in how to start and operate a business is a problem that can be corrected through education. However, the access to capital is another huge barrier. Subordinate groups who want to start their own businesses must jump through more red tape to get a loan from banks and financial institutions who issue higher interest rates.

Subordinate groups need to invest and support each other businesses. Failure to do so keep them in a state of economical slavery. When subordinate groups invest into their community, it provides jobs and keep money in the communities allowing it to roll over many times which benefit everyone. The failure to invest in their communities causes many members of the subordinate groups to live-in low-income neighborhoods where most folks are struggling to satisfy their basic needs which is turn dramatically lift the crime rate in all areas.

The racial wage gap is one of many reasons for an equally large gap in the quality of subordinate group communities, in that they have little opportunity to grow within themselves due to a lack of funds and resources. Members of subordinate groups are known to be granted "insufficient amounts and high-interest loans to start sustainable businesses or be denied altogether, whereas foreigners are awarded adequate loans, financial assistance, and low-interest rate bond financing. As a matter of fact, the U.S. Department of Commerce encourages foreign business development and opportunities in less prosperous areas by providing [foreigners] monetary aid, opposed to issuing that same assistance to members of subordinate groups that would in turn allow them to offer needed products or services in their own communities. And, it is a fact that there's preferential treatment to foreigners in federal, state, and local government assistance programs. Foreigners are also able to take advantage of the various public infrastructure and environmental loans, which unfortunately aren't readily available to blacks. And, the various state tax credits, tax refunds, or sales/use tax exemptions based on a taxpayer's satisfaction of in-state capital investment or job creation conditions allows many foreigners to sustain and grow their businesses."[cliii]

It is vitally important that members of the subordinate group are business astute. Fifty percent of all businesses do not survive in the first five years of their existence. Potential small business owners must develop well developed business and marketing plans for their businesses. A sound business plan is the key along with acquiring the necessary resources and capital. They must stay aware of the marketing conditions that exist for their type of business, the continued status of their businesses and employees and always look for ways to improve operations and efficiency.

Those who can obtain the necessary capital to fund their businesses should take calculated risk by staying ahead of the industry trends for their business. It will pay off in the long run and at the same time help revitalize and stabilize the community by provided it with the needed services and products as well as hiring people who live there.

In addition to gaining access to capital and resources, successful business owners must know how to network with other stakeholders, have a vision for their business, and have dedicated and hardworking employees. They must follow their business plans and instincts to become successful in the long run. More importantly, becoming a calculated risk taker may not be a disadvantage. Many successful business owners have gone into bankruptcy several times but persevered until they finally became successful. Also, establishing a business group to spread the risk and support each other should be a strong consideration. Finally, they must know how to market their services and products and surround themselves with the right people with the right connections. They can have the best products or services in the world but unless they market, promote and distribute them correctly, their business can still be a failure.

GENERATIONAL WEALTH STRATEGIES

Generational wealth is a major problem for the marginalized communities around the world. Many descendants from the dominant cultures had parents or grandparents were able to buy and own property and businesses or had stock market investments. They were able to pay off their properties or expand their businesses thanks to preferential treatment and employment they received from previous generational wealth. They were then able to leave the proceeds of this wealth to their children as either an inheritance or a financial 'jump-start' in life.

Most subordinate groups of the world's racial order do not have a financial 'jump-start' in life. They stand and fall on their own efforts alone and there is very little safety net if they don't make it. Their family wealth is already spread thin just to cover their basic needs. When they have financial issues, it means family debt has bottomed out and the horror of truly going under is real. When descendants of the dominant groups have financial issues, it usually means they may have to dip into their saving or investment accounts or even swallow their pride and ask their parents for help. Some are also able to receive an inheritance or life insurance that pay out a nice lump sum at some point in the life to sustain their living expenses and even save for the future and pass it on to their heirs. These are the type of financial reserves of those who have had generations of wealth pass on to their heirs. Leaving an inheritance to family members and educating them on money matters can benefit generations of family members for decades and even future centuries.

In America, Africa Americans only own one half of one percent of the wealth in the country. The dominant group has an astronomical economic lead on them. A new report published by the Center for Global Policy Solutions titled "Beyond Broke: Why Closing the Racial Wealth Gap is a Priority for National Economic Security," highlights just how drastic the contrast is between the economic security of whites and people of color.

The study revealed an unsettling truth: A full 50 years after the Civil Rights Act of 1964, economic segregation is still very much a reality in America. Maya Rockeymoore, one of the study researchers, pointed out that while Jim Crow era lynch mobs and 'white only' signs are gone, "the pernicious effects of racialized public and private institutional structures continue to operate in ways that prevent asset building or promotes asset stripping when African Americans do manage to accumulate resources."

One of the key findings of the study is that whites have 100 times more liquid wealth than blacks. Liquid wealth includes such things as cash and money held in checking accounts, bonds, or stocks. The median liquid wealth for blacks is $200 for blacks, $340 for Latinos, and $23,000 for whites.

Another key finding was in regard to tangible assets. Tangible assets include things such as homes and cars. Only six percent of whites had no tangible assets whatsoever, while 21 percent of blacks, 17 percent of Latinos, and 11 percent of Asians had no tangible assets.

The study also found that during the most recent economic recession, blacks saw their net wealth plummet by 53 percent, Latinos by 65 percent, and Asians by 54 percent, while whites only saw a decrease of 16 percent. To further illustrate just how significant the racial wealth gap is, for every dollar that whites own, blacks own six cents, and Latinos own 7 cents.[cliv]

Many Africa Americans lives are poorer compared to other citizens due to the legacy of slavery, Jim Crow laws and public policies which were symptoms of institutional racism. One way to change the wealth disparity will be through public policy initiatives. For example, from 1935 to 1968, ninety-eight percent of all Federal Housing Administration (FHA) mortgage loans were given out to members of the dominant culture. Historically, the majority of generational wealth is tied to home ownership. Since African Americans weren't allowed access to the GI bill in the 1940's after World War II, they would be in a much better position with home ownership and wealth. Instead, many were redlined to the inner cities living in the inner cities, ghettos and projects.

One of the most effective tools used to control subordinate groups is the denial of access to economic resources. The number one cure for racism is financial independence. If they closely study the history of people of color's oppression (past and present), they will notice it's largely centered around a lack of generational wealth. Business and home ownerships as well as long term investment in the stock market are the keys to financial success. In this global economy, financial independence and stability will gain them instant respect from other groups and a major hurdle in breaking down barriers between the racial groups.

POLITICAL STRATEGIES

Moreover, the subordinate groups must continue to become more political astute and savvy. Politics always matter. They must understand how government works and particularly the political dynamics that are involved. It will enable the subordinate groups to work well with people in power and in turn they can use their power and influence to help marginalized and disenfranchised communities. It is a matter of knowing how to work with the powers to be. It will enable them to get what they need for their communities and know what they can do for themselves. Being politically astute involves knowing how power resides in the various structures of a political entity at the different levels of government.

Politicians and career government officials often make decisions on issues that affect their way of life and the communities they live in. "Fundamental to dismantling racism is helping individuals who are part of an organization to recognize how organizations utilize power to create, perpetuate, and maintain power inequities".[clv]

In addition to understanding how politics and power reside and how it is derived, it is important to know how it is maintained. Power is exercised by the dominant culture through overt decision making, agenda setting and prioritization, and shaping meaning, ideology and worldview. It is important that subordinate group members understand how and what decisions are made, the power inherent in deciding what should be on an agenda for discussion, and how the issues on the agenda are prioritized. It is also critical for subordinate members to learn how issues are shaped and framed for discussion involving ideologies and worldviews that serve as the context for decisions.[clvi]

It is also important if subordinate group members are informed voters and occupy political positions within their political entities. Many marginalized communities are powerless or have little voice in the halls of power. Therefore, they rarely change the basic makeup and outcomes of their communities. At the minimum, individuals should become part of the political process by at least expressing their rights to vote in every single election as there is no greater responsibility in being in control of your destiny. As a group, they should stay energized and galvanized to ensure their voices are heard by utilizing the voting booths to place people in office who will take on critical issues and have their best interest in mind.

THE CHRUCH

In marginalized communities throughout the world, the church has always been the stabilizing force of subordinate groups beginning with slavery and throughout the post-civil rights era until today. The church played a very prominent role in the civil rights era under the leadership of Dr. Martin Luther King Jr., Nelson Mandela and other prominent civil rights leader in implementing the agenda in creating a more just global society. Many of the leaders of the movement were pastors in their churches. The church not only offered support but provided an organizational base for meetings and to plan strategies to overcome their adversities.

The subordinate groups could always count on the church as a sanctuary even in some of the lowest point in their history. Many of these churches have not only been involved in traditional religious matters such as providing spiritual and emotional needs, worship, fellowship, missionary outreach, helping the sick and elderly, providing meals for the needed, counseling members, and assisting members when disasters occur but they have essentially also operated as non-governmental social agency.

In many instances, churches have also provided services to their communities that traditional local government agencies have provided in the past. Churches have partnered with many stakeholders to provide needed services for their members and others in their communities. Many provide numerous outreach efforts in areas such health care, educational workshops, youth clubs, gang violence workshops, prison outreach, child care, financial planning, tax preparation, job fairs, voting precincts, etc.

The church has been able to bring marginalized communities together and have recently taken on an ever-increasing expanded role to address chronic societal issues that resulted from the world racial order. Today, the church continues to play a major role in changing our society.

CONCLUSION

Although the aforementioned strategies, if implemented, can help the world minimize racism on a global scale, there are still many parts of the world where subordinate group members live, and their country's governments are not as conducive to a fair and just society. Many of these countries are located in Asia, South American, Central American and the Middle East and even some parts of Europe. These countries have no programs or agencies charged with defending the civil and human rights of the subordinate group members. Even if subordinate group members protested their conditions and treatment by the dominant culture group, there are no laws or penalties to protect them from racism. However, a country can make rules and laws against racial discrimination, but that still may not change peoples' attitudes. Unfortunately, many of these subordinate group members still experience regular biases and have reluctantly accepted their lot in life. Very few of their members are in political positions or positions of power. Most are still confined to menial jobs and live in deplorable living conditions.

Although racial progress has been made in many parts of the world during the past few decades, there are still many pockets of resistance and some countries still tote the racial status quo which has existed for centuries. That is why I mentioned in the Introduction that finding strategies for global justice would not be easy. It is due to an unequal world racial order that presently exist. Subordinate members in those countries will face additional challenges and barriers in their quest to achieve global racial justice. Also, it will also take them longer as a group to achieve global racial justice.

Since the dominant group governs the countries and ensure their power privileges are maintained, the subordinate group members are still powerless in those societies. However, it has not stopped many subordinate groups from at least forming human and civil rights groups in recent years. Hopefully, forming these groups and partnering with other stakeholders will be the first steps of a long journey to achieving racial equality in those countries.

Worldwide, subordinate group members continue to practice vagility and migrate to other countries who they feel are more amendable to their human and civil rights. "Millions are on the move from impoverished rural areas to cities, and from poorer countries to wealthier ones, in search of work. Migrants are especially vulnerable—they are often very far from home, don't speak the local language, have no funds to return home, and have no friends or family to rely on." [clvii]

In some instances, many lacks the resources to migrate to other countries not only to escape racial issues but also socioeconomic reasons such as poverty and crime that resulted from racism. However, some subordinate groups become so desperate to find a better way of life that they still migrate to other countries at any cause. However, in recent decades, some countries in Europe and America have tighten their immigration laws to discourage them from migrating. Even those who are successful in migrating to countries more amenable to human rights compared to the native countries, some still experience racism, discrimination and biases in their new countries.

If transformative forces persist and prevail, the United States and the world can finally move toward becoming the world society that United States President James Madison and one of the nation's founding fathers envisioned in Federalist #10 (The Article of Confederation). He imagined a society in which no majority faction, not even native-born European Americans, dominates the political, economic, or social arena.

The Madisonian vision must not blind us to two concerns. If it persists, the world racial order will not have only beneficial results. Some subordinate members are likely to be harmed by these changes and will thereby suffer relative or even absolute losses. Continuing the venerable American pattern, they will be disproportionately African American or Native American, supplemented by undocumented immigrants. All Americans are likely to lose some of the joys and advantages of a strong sense of group identity and rootedness.

The greater concern, however, is that the world racial order will not persist and prevail. Subordinate groups' poverty and alienation may be too deep; dominant culture may be too tenacious; institutional change may be too shallow; undocumented immigrants may not attain a path to belonging; genomic research may usher in a new era of eugenic discrimination. In short, Americans and the world may in the end lack the political will to finish what demographic change, scientific research, young adults' worldviews, and the momentum of the past decade have started.[clviii]

President James Madison believed that people are by nature diverse and self-interested, and thus every society form faction, or groups of people with special interests that sometimes harm other citizens or the good of the whole. Under one centralized representative government, a diverse nation could thrive, ruled by the majority, but with a fair amount of consideration for all.[clix]

It is very ironic that many founders of the United States Constitution, some of whom later would become Presidents of the United States, including Presidents George Washington, James Madison and Thomas Jefferson were slave owners. Yet some of their views expressed in the nation's document were inconsistent in denying the freedom and liberty to the African slaves, the indigenous people and women. They also didn't match their actions in private life due to their own practice of slavery. Nor did they later use their broad presidential persuasion powers in working with Congress when they became President to steer the country in another direction to end the contradictions. This inaction decades later led to the United States Civil War that ended the institution of slavery and took us to this point in world's history in which the legacy of global racism continues today.

During the past few decades, we have evolved as a global society. It just has not happen as quickly as decency would demand. Even the global major transformational events during the past century took several decades to effectively dismantle them and we are still experiencing lingering residues of racial hostilities. The doctrine of racial superiority and inferiority ideology has been around for hundreds of years and some descendants of their champions are still with us. But the institution of racism based solely on one attribute of a person's genetic makeup is diminishing decade by decade. As unfair as it is for anyone to have to wait for simple justice and equality, I know that in practice, it often takes longer than it should.

Human beings have survived because of the creation of learned shared social cultures that is transmitted from one generation to the next. Several other past Earth's inhabitants became extinct due to natural catastrophes and disasters, interbreeding, inability to cope with nature, among other factors. Human beings in general appear to have the intelligence and mental ability to cope with nature and endure it, but do we have the will to get along with our fellow human beings? It appears that some members of the human race still have a vested interest in eliminating their own members through wars and genocide due to culture and religion differences and racism based on physical attributes and characteristics.

On the other hand, through the mixing of the racial groups, human beings are creating new cultures and ethnicities that begun when the dominant culture decided to conquer other racial groups through world-wide Colonization, slavery and the genocide of indigenous people five centuries ago. Human beings have always practice vagility throughout history thereby increasing immigration and multi-culturalism worldwide. If this pattern continues among human beings over the next few centuries, there will not be any subordinate racial groups to feel superior to. There will not be a need for dominant culture groups to invade and conquer other racial groups. All racial groups will be involved in the world's strategic plan and have input in the sharing of power of the globe's destiny. The 'survival of the fittest' concept pertaining to the human beings will then be irrelevant. This will then become the natural order of the universe.

A final view of this complex, global social phenomenon is that these may the last desperate gasps of a dying deranged ideology of racial superiority and inferiority seeking to cling to a past that cannot pass through the gates of multi-cultural future. It is difficult to see the death of racism in the short time that we are afforded in our lives and maybe it never fully dies. But it appears that we may be standing in the twilights of a dying culture and society. Furthermore, the strides and progress that have been made by subordinate groups are meaningful and significant in view of the world's major racial transformation events of the last few decades. While I am troubled, I am also confident that change will come. It cannot be stopped. My confidence is not simply hope.

It is based on compelling historical evidence from past great empires, civilizations and societies that nothing lasts forever and the existing dominant culture either must reinvent itself or collapse and suffer an ending date. There is also a supreme confidence in the sense that these social ills that plague the world are subject to natural evolutionary processes and the fights against nature are futile. The tolerance reservoir has run out and the reservoir is getting shallower. Why would any racial group act to perpetuate servitude by another racial group? While it may appear as such on the surface, they are just in a survival mode until the subordinate racial groups break free. Some members may not make it, and some may even die in the process, but while in the net, the subordinate groups must survive.

The subordinate groups around the world must continue to push for change as global racism requires constant maintenance or behaviors and attitudes will not change. As migration and vagility increase worldwide, the dominant group's denial is challenged and the understanding of racism increases, the global prominence of racism will ultimately decrease.[clx] The subordinate groups must continue to challenge the dominant group culture until its attitudes and behaviors based solely on one attribute of a person's genetic makeup and lineage begin to change permanently.

As human beings, we can lament the horrors of the past, recognize the pain of the present, and still hope for a far more glorious global future. In retrospect, the plight of subordinate groups has come full circle. The trials and tribulations that their ancestors experience have been a bridge that their descendants have also had to cross, albeit to a lesser extent. Sometimes a situation that seems to be hopeless and broken forever finds a way to be renewed. Now we are seeing the human embodiment of their descendant's spirits that has been revived since the recent global racial transformational events. The long-term suffering experienced by their ancestors did not end fast enough in their lifetimes. For many subordinate group members, alive and deceased, it has been a long five-hundred-year struggle. However, the arc of history for their descendants is long, but it keeps swinging in the direction of progress and bends towards global racial justice. On a global scale, this is where we are today in racial reconciliation.